the guide to a
GLUTEN-FREE
DIET

*One in six people are suffering from a serious illness that has a safe,
effective, and inexpensive remedy: avoiding gluten.*

David Brownstein, M.D. & Sheryl Shenefelt, C.N.

For further copies of *The Guide to a Gluten-Free Diet:*

Order online: www.drbrownstein.com or www.aplacetobe.com

Call: **1-888-647-5616** or send a check or money order in the amount of: $19.00 ($15.00 plus $5.00 shipping and handling), or for Michigan residents $19.90 ($15.00 plus $5.00 shipping and handling, plus $.90 sales tax) to:

> Healthy Living
> 964 Floyd Street
> Birmingham, Michigan 48009

The Guide to a Gluten-Free Diet
Cover Design by AshleyCazaCreative
Copyright © 2008
by David Brownstein, M.D. and Sheryl Shenefelt, C.N.
All Rights Reserved
No part of this book may be reproduced without written consent from the publisher.

ISBN: 978-0-9660882-8-1
Healthy Living
964 Floyd Street
Birmingham, Michigan 48009
(248) 851-3372
(888) 647-5616

Center for Holistic Medicine
(248) 851-1600

A Place to Be, LLC
(248) 766-2425

Acknowledgements

David Brownstein, M.D.

I gratefully acknowledge the help I have received from my friends and colleagues in putting this book together. This book could not have been published without help from the editors— my wife, Allison and my chief editor, Janet Darnell.

Of course, to my patients THANK YOU! Without your support and search for safe and effective natural treatments, none of this would be possible. I believe in you and I thank you for believing in me.

Sheryl Shenefelt, C.N.

I want to express my deep gratitude to my family for their unwavering support as I pursue my passion of health and wellness. I am honored to write this book with Dr. David Brownstein and work with him and his partners at The Center for Holistic Medicine. Thank you, also, to all of my patients, newsletter readers, and class attendees for believing in me. I also appreciate the work of The Tri-County Celiac Support Group, for all of the great resources, such as the shopping guide, that have helped me learn about gluten-free living.

How to Utilize this Book

The following questions will be answered:

- ➢ What does gluten-free mean?

- ➢ What foods can I eat if I am gluten-free?

- ➢ How do I shop for gluten-free products?

More and more information is becoming available about eating gluten-free as people are realizing the connection between diet and health. Gluten-free is a lifestyle many are adopting even if they have never been diagnosed with celiac disease. Many people have digestive complaints, allergies, bloating, fatigue, autoimmune conditions, or other symptoms that are leading them to incorporate a gluten-free lifestyle.

This book is meant to serve as a guide to developing a gluten-free lifestyle. Research and frequently asked questions about what being "gluten-free" entails is given, along with suggestions, ideas, and recipes to help you with your journey. It is always important to ask questions and read labels each time you make a purchase or plan to eat something to ensure it is, in fact, gluten-free. Joining groups or organizations such as those listed in Appendix A can be helpful on your journey. Often gluten is hidden in items we would not think to check such as medications or shampoo. As a health conscious consumer, it is important that we get in the habit of calling manufacturers and food producers to research their products so that our families will be safe from unknown sources of gluten. Many products that you think to be gluten-free one day, may not be the next. Many companies change ingredients in their products throughout the year. Use this book to get ideas, to guide you in your transition, and for resources with your new gluten-free lifestyle.

A Word of Caution to the Reader

The information presented in this book is based on the training and professional experience of the authors. The advice in this book should not be undertaken without first consulting a physician. Proper laboratory and clinical monitoring is essential to achieving the goals of finding safe and effective natural treatments. This book was written for informational and educational purposes only. It is not intended to be used as medical advice.

Dedications

David Brownstein, M.D.

To the women of my life: Allison, Hailey and Jessica, with all my love.

Sheryl Shenefelt, C.N.

All my love to my wonderful husband Bob and to my beautiful children Grace and Nicholas for all of their support and patience.

Contents

Preface   1

Chapter 1:   Understanding Gluten   17

Chapter 2:   Celiac Disease   29

Chapter 3:   Why Avoid Gluten?   39

Chapter 4:   Gluten, The Thyroid, and Autoimmune Disorders 51

Chapter 5:   Gluten and Bowel Disorders   65

Chapter 6:   Transitioning to a Gluten-Free Lifestyle   73

Chapter 7:   Eating Out and Staying Gluten-Free   89

Chapter 8:   Children and a Gluten-Free Lifestyle   99

Chapter 9:   Cooking and Preparing Gluten-Free   109

Chapter 10: Gluten-Free Meal Ideas, Tips, and Recipes   117

Appendix A: Celiac Disease and
                    Other Gluten-Free Resources   149

Appendix B: Gluten-Free Start-Up Shopping Guide   157

Appendix C: Restaurant Guide   159

About the Authors   161

Preface
David Brownstein, M.D.

Sheryl and I wrote this book to help the reader find information on how to eat a healthier diet. We are facing unprecedented illness in our country. More and more people are getting cancer, autoimmune disorders, arthritis, thyroid disorders, heart disease, and other chronic illnesses than ever before. There is no doubt that dietary patterns are, in part, to blame for the growing number of serious illnesses. When I was in medical school, there was little mentioned about diet. We were led to believe that there was little or no relationship between diet and the development of most diseases.

After practicing medicine for nearly 12 years, I know there is a relationship between one's dietary choices and their ability to either be healthy or ill. I have seen wonderful changes in a patient's disease pattern when they adopt a healthier diet. I have witnessed the cure of many chronic illnesses, which I was taught had no cure, with the adoption of a healthy diet. I am certain that our dietary choices affect us down to our core being.

The good news is, if we eat a healthy diet, we can give our bodies the best chance to achieve optimal health. Many times, this just requires a little education to learn which foods supply the best nutrients for our bodies. That is why Sheryl and I wrote this book, as well as our other book **The Guide to Healthy Eating** - to give you the knowledge to make better food choices.

So, why eat a gluten-free diet? Over 1 percent of the U.S. population currently suffers from celiac disease and 97 percent of those patients are not being diagnosed. I believe a much larger percentage, from 20-30 percent of our population, currently suffers from gluten sensitivity and could benefit from eating a gluten-free, or at least a gluten-lowered diet. Over one-third of our population is obese. We have diabetes occurring at epidemic levels. Obesity and diabetes are directly related to dietary choices. All people suffering from diabetes and obesity deserve a trial of becoming gluten-free. I have seen wonderful results in my patients who suffer with these disorders when they become gluten-free.

This book was written to give you direction and hope. You can overcome chronic illness. You can achieve your optimal health. However, you have to take the steps to accomplish these tasks. You have to eat a healthy diet. Eating a gluten-free diet can have remarkable positive effects on your health.

TO ALL OF OUR HEALTH!

Sheryl Shenefelt, C.N.

I became interested in allergies, healthy eating, and gluten-free diets when my daughter began having symptoms of what might have been asthma and allergies. She was about six-months-old. Our pediatrician said because of her continuous cough and excessive tearing from one eye, he recommended a chest x-ray. He also prescribed Zantac with the possibility of later adding Albuterol after the x-ray "in case" she might have allergies or asthma. He said he wanted to see what happened and whether the condition would clear up or not. Of course, I was opposed to exposing my six-month-old daughter to x-rays and speculative treatments unless she had a life threatening condition. I knew for sure that the medications were not going to get to the root of her issues. This began a long journey using homeopathic and natural treatments, food elimination diets including a gluten-free diet, and food rotation diets. Over time, I could see clear changes in her behavior, speech, communication skills, allergies, and overall demeanor depending on what she had to eat on any given day. When she was one year old, I had an extreme wake up call about food and the immediate impact it can have on an individual. My daughter leaned over and dipped her apple in some of my peanut butter which brought an extreme allergic reaction -- gasping for breath, hives, and swelling around the eyes in just a matter of a few minutes. That's when I knew without a doubt how much of an impact food has on our bodies and our health. Grace is now 6 years old and is able to tolerate many foods (other than peanuts); however, if we have an excess of anything or if we have too many "fake foods", processed foods, or foods with chemicals (i.e., red dye number 5), it may trigger reactions like coughing or congestion. Our family now eats mainly gluten-free items. We also refer to The Weston A. Price Foundation www.westonaprice.org as a valued resource for education in healthy dietary practices. For example, we use the recommended soaking methods this group promotes to ease in the digestibility of grains, which allows us to still incorporate certain grain items. But through our journey we have had periods where we have been completely gluten-free (not even soaked). To those that have to avoid gluten every day, my advice is to take it one day at a time, find replacements you can live with, and find a support group or network of others eating the same way. I have found that, as time has passed, it is easier for me and my family to be gluten-free because it is what we are familiar with now, just as we were familiar before with eating wheat products. We choose to be gluten-free now because we have seen the benefits, and though we do not necessarily have a "celiac diagnosis" or a doctor telling us to be gluten-free, we know it is the best thing for our family at this time.

1

Understanding Gluten

Introduction

Gluten sensitivity and gluten-free diets are becoming more and more common. This chapter will give you an overview of gluten, which is a protein found in many grains. Gluten is associated with many symptoms and many diseases. Keep in mind, oftentimes people who are sensitive to gluten may not have any symptoms or digestive issues relating to the intestinal tract. As you learn more about gluten you will be able to pick out which foods to eat and which foods to avoid and begin transitioning to a gluten-free lifestyle.

Frequently Asked Questions

What Is Gluten?

Gluten is the name of a series of proteins found in many different grains such as wheat, barley, and rye. Table 1 gives examples of gluten-containing grains.

Gluten is a very difficult-to-digest protein. Human beings have only been exposed to gluten-containing grains as a major part of their diets for approximately 12,000 years. We have been eating other foods such as meats, fruits, and vegetables for approximately 2.5 million years.[1] You can see that the consumption of grains as a major part of our diet has not been around a long time on the evolutionary time scale. Moreover, the grains today are much different than grains from the past. Hybridization, as well as chemical processing, have altered the nutritional content of grains, and this may be why more and more cases of gluten sensitivity and celiac disease are now arising at increasing rates.

Table 1: Gluten-Containing Grains

Barley	Semolina
Bulgur	Spelt
Couscous	Triticale
Durum	Rye
Einkorn	Wheat bran
Kamut	Wheat germ
Malt	Wheat starch

Do Oats Contain Gluten?

Yes and no. Inherently, oats do not necessarily contain gluten; but, they are often processed with wheat and become contaminated. Unless they are guaranteed to be uncontaminated, they need to be avoided.

Why Is Gluten Used In So Many Products?

Gluten is used in many baking products to help the item rise (leavening agent) and for its ability to form the structure of dough which holds products together. Gluten can also be found in many commonly added ingredients as listed in Table 2 below. Chapter 6 contains more detailed lists of items containing gluten.

Table 2: Ingredients Which May Contain Gluten

Dextrin
Hydrolyzed plant or vegetable protein (HPP or HVP)
Maltodextrin
Monosodium glutamate (MSG)
Seasoning and flavoring products
Starch (modified food starch)
Textured plant or vegetable protein (TPP or TVP)

Why Should Someone Avoid Gluten?

Celiac disease is a diagnosis given after a biopsy of the small intestine reveals a particular pattern of damage due to gluten ingestion. Those with this diagnosis are the only patients recommended to become gluten-free in conventional medicine. More about celiac disease will be found in Chapter 2.

Celiac disease patients, however, are not the only category of patients that would benefit from a gluten-free diet. You can also have sensitivity to gluten that is not picked up by either a biopsy of the small intestine or blood testing. This is known as non-celiac gluten sensitivity. Celiac disease and non-celiac gluten sensitivity are both associated with a host of serious illnesses as shown in Table 4 (Chapter 3, p. 44). For the purposes of this book, the term "gluten sensitivity" will encompass both celiac disease and non-celiac gluten sensitivity.

Non-celiac gluten sensitivity will be discussed more in Chapter 3. It is affecting millions of people today. In our experience, people with autoimmune illnesses as well as many patients diagnosed with chronic health conditions in Table 4 (Chapter 3, p. 44) often find relief from avoiding gluten. See Chapter 6 for foods to avoid and foods that can be eaten on a gluten-free diet.

If I Have Never Had A Problem After Eating Gluten, Do I Need To Avoid It?

Not necessarily, although our experience has shown that most people feel better while avoiding gluten. Remember, gluten sensitivity may not show up with an immediate or even obvious reaction to gluten. There may not even be any digestive symptoms such as discomfort, diarrhea, bloating, gas, or constipation. Our experience has shown that eating a large amount of gluten in the diet predisposes one to digestive problems as well as an increased tendency to gain weight.

Why Are People Sensitive To Gluten?

Many people have poor eating habits, leading to digestive issues, which results in gluten and other proteins not being properly digested.

Over time, poor digestion results in damage to the little finger-like protrusions in the small intestine--the villi. Furthermore, many people have a genetic predisposition for celiac disease, as well as gluten sensitivity.

The villi are important as this is where the nutrients from food are digested and absorbed. If enough villi are damaged from ingesting gluten, the nutrients from food are unable to be absorbed. This can result in a state of malnourishment.

Another issue that can arise with gluten sensitivity is called leaky gut syndrome. Leaky gut syndrome occurs when particles of foods actually begin to leak into the blood stream, causing the immune system to overreact. More on leaky gut syndrome can be found in Chapter 4.

What If I Am Gluten Sensitive, But I Keep Ingesting Gluten?

For those who are gluten sensitive, the long-term ingestion of gluten-containing grains can cause later development of many serious health problems including: autoimmune disorders, infertility, cancer, thyroid diseases, and even death. More about gluten sensitivity and the illnesses associated with it can be found in Chapter 3.

How Long Should Someone Be On A Gluten-Free Diet?

The ingestion of gluten-containing products can provoke many adverse health reactions in someone who has gluten sensitivity. If you have any of the symptoms listed in Table 3 (Chapter 2, p. 35) or any of the illnesses listed in Table 4 (Chapter 3, p. 44), a serious consideration should be given to becoming gluten-free. If you have been diagnosed with celiac disease (see Chapter 2), then you will need to have a lifelong adherence to a gluten-free diet.

Remember, you must become gluten-free for at least six weeks (without cheating) to gauge the effects of gluten. Even just a bite or two here and there is not a "gluten-free diet," because gluten has a cumulative effect and the immune system can react for up to six weeks after being exposed to gluten.

It may seem daunting to become gluten-free, but with a little education and elbow grease, it can be accomplished. See Chapter 6, "Transitioning to a Gluten-Free Diet", for tips.

Could Someone Ever Tolerate Gluten Again In Their Diet After Going Gluten-Free?

This is not an easy question to answer. In our experience, many people with chronic health conditions improve on a gluten-free diet. Additionally, even those patients without a diagnosis contained in Table 4 (Chapter 3, p. 44) generally feel better when avoiding wheat and gluten. In our experience, there is an added benefit to going gluten-free for most people—they have an enhanced ability to lose weight.

Do You Have To Avoid Gluten For The Rest Of Your Life?

That depends. If you become gluten-free for six weeks and notice no substantial benefits to your health, then perhaps it is not necessary for you to maintain a gluten-free diet.

We recommend in this case that you use a gluten-free diet in moderation and also try using proper grain preparation as taught by the Weston A. Price Foundation, including soaking grains to help with the tolerance and proper digestion of gluten. However, a positive change in your health will provide you with the answer you need - stay gluten-free. Depending on your situation, you and your health care provider will need to decide what type of diet or lifestyle modifications are best for you. For more resources and information on soaking grains please visit www.westonaprice.org.

Final Thoughts

This chapter explored what gluten is and some of the reasons to avoid gluten. If you think you are sensitive to gluten or if you want to find out if you are sensitive to gluten, then we recommend trying a gluten-free diet for a minimum of six weeks. If any symptoms you may have been having improve during this trial, then you have your answer – you are sensitive to gluten and should continue on with a gluten-free diet.

[1] Braly, J and Hoggan, M. Dangerous Grains. 2002. Penguin Group.

2

Celiac Disease

Introduction

What would you say if there was a serious illness currently affecting approximately 1 percent of the worldwide population, and about 3 million Americans that is only rarely diagnosed? What if 97 percent of the people with this illness, some suffering from serious autoimmune disorders, cancers, and early death, were not being diagnosed or being misdiagnosed? Furthermore, what would you say if this illness, once diagnosed, had a simple, safe, and inexpensive remedy to it that did not require the use of a pharmaceutical drug?

Surprisingly, in 2007, this illness and its safe and effective remedy does exist. The illness is celiac disease. If you are diagnosed with celiac disease, the safe and effective treatment is to avoid the protein gluten in your diet. This dietary change is nearly 100 percent effective in everyone who adheres to it.

Frequently Asked Questions

What Is Celiac Disease?

Celiac disease is an autoimmune digestive disease that results in damage to the small intestine. It is defined as a permanent intolerance to ingested gluten that results in immunologically mediated inflammatory damage to the small intestine mucosa.[1]

In simpler terms, to a patient with celiac disease, gluten is a poison. The ingestion of gluten in a celiac patient will result in the immune system becoming activated. These immune cells produce antibodies against gluten and the antibodies damage the sensitive tissue of the small intestine—the villi. The villi are the finger-like projections in the small intestine that are responsible for absorbing nutrients from your diet. Celiac disease is woefully underdiagnosed and frequently misdiagnosed. Even in today's modern world, millions of people needlessly suffer from celiac disease. We believe it is the most commonly missed diagnosis present today.

Celiac disease is classified as an autoimmune illness. The reaction to ingesting gluten causes the body's own immune system to damage the villi of the small intestine. More about autoimmune illnesses can be found in Chapter 4.

How Is Celiac Disease Diagnosed?

In conventional medicine, celiac disease is a diagnosis given when there has been a biopsy of the small bowel which shows lack of villi.[2] In addition, extremely sensitive and specific laboratory tests exist which test the serum and are giving reliable information toward the diagnosis of celiac disease.

Today, there are even more advanced technologies such as one by EnteroLab, which utilizes stool samples to test for antibodies in gluten sensitive individuals. Another was reported in the American Journal of Gastroenterology, called a video capsule enteroscopy (VCE), which can accurately detect intestinal atrophy in patients suspected to have celiac disease.

There has been a lot of research pinpointing undiagnosed celiac disease with the later development of long-term health conditions. Therefore, it is particularly important to work with a health care practitioner familiar with the various aspects of both celiac disease and non-celiac gluten sensitivity. Both illnesses are similarly treated; remove gluten from the diet.

If An Intestinal Biopsy Shows Up Negative, Can I Tolerate Gluten?

Unfortunately, the answer to this question is no. Recent research points out that an intestinal biopsy often fails to show any signs of damage to the villi even when gluten sensitivity is present. The reaction to gluten may show up in many different ways. Some people complain of irritable bowel symptoms such as alternating diarrhea and constipation. Others may be diagnosed with an autoimmune disorder and have tissue damage outside of the gastrointestinal tract. Chapter 4 will explore the link between gluten sensitivity and seemingly unrelated illnesses including thyroid and autoimmune illnesses.

What Are The Symptoms Of Celiac Disease?

The symptoms of celiac disease can vary. Many physicians feel that gastrointestinal symptoms (particularly diarrhea and bloating) are the only true signs of celiac disease. Research has clearly shown that celiac disease can affect nearly every system in the body, including the gastrointestinal tract.[3] Some of the symptoms of celiac disease are listed in Table 3.

Table 3: Symptoms of Celiac Disease

Abdominal pain
Amenorrhea (no menstrual periods)
Anemia
Apthous ulcers (canker sores)
Behavioral changes
Bloating
Bone or joint pain
Chronic diarrhea
Constipation
Delayed growth
Dermatitis herpetiformis
Failure to thrive in infants
Fatigue
Infertility
Lactose intolerance
Loss of enamel on teeth
Migraines
Muscle cramps

If I Have Any Of The Symptoms Listed In Table 3, Do I Have Celiac Disease?

Just because you have one or more of these symptoms does not necessarily mean you have celiac disease. There is no predominant symptom associated with celiac disease. The symptoms listed in Table 3 are very broad. In fact, these symptoms are the same for some of the most common diseases affecting millions of people. Any of these symptoms can be present with or without bowel involvement in celiac disease.[4] If you suffer from any of the symptoms listed in Table 3, we suggest you consider a gluten-free trial to see if your symptoms improve. More about making your diet gluten-free is covered in Chapter 6.

What Are The Treatments For Celiac Disease?

The only true treatment for celiac disease is the strict adherence to a gluten-free diet. The good news is that there is no expensive pharmaceutical pill (full of adverse effects) that you can take for this disease. Total withdrawal of gluten from the diet permits the intestines to heal.

In fact, becoming gluten-free will allow the damaged villi to repair themselves and resume their normal function. For a celiac patient, even after this occurs, it is important to remain permanently on a gluten-free diet, although symptoms may disappear.

Final Thoughts

Celiac disease is a common illness that is not being correctly diagnosed in 97 percent of those individuals suffering from it. It is important for you to educate yourself about gluten sensitivity and its solution. The remedy for celiac disease is simple, safe and effective - avoid gluten. For celiac disease and gluten-free resources, please see Appendix A.

[1] Am. J. Clin. Nutr. 1999. Mar;69(3)354-65

[2] BMJ. 2005. Apr2:330(7494):739-40

[3] From National Institute of Health. Nih.gov/ddiseases/pubs/celiac accessed 7.3.07

[4] BMJ. 2005. Apr. 2;330(7494)775-6

3

Why Avoid Gluten?

Introduction

Gluten sensitivity (including celiac disease) can cause a whole host of immune system problems. As mentioned in the first chapter, gluten is a protein found in many grain products (e.g., wheat, barley, rye, and related grains of spelt, kamut, and triticale). For those that are sensitive to gluten, its ingestion can lead to the immune system attacking itself, and to the development of many serious illnesses including: autoimmune illnesses, cancer, chronic fatigue syndrome, and arthritis. This chapter will review how gluten can negatively affect the body, and what the consequences of ingesting gluten are if you happen to be sensitive to it.

Frequently Asked Questions

How Common Is Gluten Sensitivity?

Gluten sensitivity is extremely common. The numbers of people suffering with this illness are staggering. There are estimates that nearly 1 in 133 Americans suffer from celiac disease (with perhaps one in six having gluten sensitivity). As previously stated, only about 1-3 percent of those with the illness are being properly diagnosed. That means that approximately 97-99 percent of patients with celiac disease or gluten sensitivity are not being diagnosed.

What Does Gluten Do To People That Are Sensitive To It?

For those that are unable to properly digest gluten, ingesting it can be a disaster for the body and the immune system. Food that is properly digested in the stomach is sent to the small intestine for the absorption of the nutrients in the food. This absorption occurs at a site in the small intestine called the villi.

This is where vitamins, minerals, and other nutrients are absorbed. If this area is damaged, the body is unable to properly absorb nutrients from food. Long-term damage to the villi will inevitably lead to a malnourished state.

What Illnesses Are Associated With Ingesting Gluten?

As previously mentioned, when someone who has gluten sensitivity ingests gluten, the immune system reacts by producing antibodies against gluten. These antibodies will damage the villi of the small intestine. If a gluten-sensitive individual continues to ingest gluten, the small intestine is continually assaulted. This will lead to a decline in intestinal function often characterized by bloating and diarrhea. Also, this can lead to a leaky gut. See Chapter 4 for more information on leaky gut syndrome.

Sometimes intestinal damage does not occur, but damage is done elsewhere in the body from the ingestion of gluten.

This will often be missed by a doctor who only looks for damaged villi as the clue to gluten sensitivity. This damage elsewhere can take nearly any form including damage to the organs or the connective tissue. Table 4 gives some examples of illnesses associated with gluten sensitivity. The long-term damage from gluten sensitivity can be immense and deadly.

Table 4: Illnesses Associated With Gluten Sensitivity

ADD/ADHD
Autism
Autoimmune Disorders
Asthma
Cancer
Cerebellar ataxia
Crohn's Disease
Children with
    learning disabilities
Chronic liver disease
    (including primary
        biliary cirrhosis)
Depression
Diabetics and first-degree
    relatives with insulin-
    dependent diabetes

Irritable bowel
Infertility
Iron deficiency
    anemia
Gastroesophageal
    reflux
Graves' disease
Hashimoto's disease
Headaches
Insulin-dependent
    diabetes
Migraines
Obesity
Osteoporosis
Peripheral
    neuropathy
Seizures

Is Every Diagnosis In Table 4 Due To Gluten Sensitivity?

No, Table 4 does not imply that every diagnosis contained there is solely due to gluten sensitivity. It also does not imply that every patient with a diagnosis contained in Table 4 will be gluten sensitive. However, every patient with a diagnosis contained in Table 4 should be checked for gluten sensitivity. This can be done initially through common blood testing or, better yet, through a therapeutic trial of becoming gluten-free. Chapter 6 will give you examples of foods that you can safely use in a gluten-free dietary trial. Furthermore, Chapters 4 and 5 will go into more detail about the illnesses associated with gluten sensitivity.

Why Hasn't My Doctor Checked Me For A Gluten Sensitivity Or Allergy?

The answer to the above question is so simple many cannot see it. The treatment for gluten sensitivity does not require an expensive drug regimen (which has multiple side effects, by the way).

The treatment is very simple, safe, and effective: change your diet and avoid gluten.

The pharmaceutical industry, known as Big Pharma, has no real interest in treating any of the illnesses listed in Table 4 with dietary changes. Their goal is to use expensive drug therapies that people have to take for long time periods. Most of the money allocated for physician training comes from Big Pharma. Doctors are given only brief training in diet therapies. There is a very good chance your doctor does not even know of the correlation between many different illnesses and gluten sensitivity. In fact, if you do not have severe diarrhea, it is a good bet that your doctor will not think of a food allergy as the source of your illness. However, our experience has been clear: food allergies and intolerances are a common underlying cause or aggravator of many illnesses, including all of the illnesses shown in Table 4. Unless the food allergy or intolerance is searched for and either eliminated or treated, many times the illness will continue to progress.

Why Hasn't Gluten Sensitivity Been More Widely Recognized?

You would think it would be more commonly recognized, considering that around one out of every six people has a gluten-sensitivity problem. You would think that since it causes serious and life-threatening illnesses, and there is a proven safe and inexpensive remedy, many doctors and organizations would be ecstatic and spreading the word. However, it is not always that easy; you need to follow the money. As previously mentioned, a diagnosis of gluten sensitivity or celiac disease does not require an expensive drug therapy regimen to correct it. Unfortunately, in today's world, Big Pharma controls nearly all of the medical information going to consumers and physicians. Most of the research being undertaken today has to do with expensive drug therapies. If there is no drug to treat a specific illness (as is the case with gluten sensitivity or celiac disease), Big Pharma will have no interest in educating doctors or consumers on the therapy. That is why it is so important to educate yourself about safe and effective natural therapies that are available for you.

Why Is The Intestinal Biopsy Missing So Many Cases Of Celiac Disease?

Gluten may cause problems in two ways. It may cause a direct irritation to the lining of the small bowel. This may lead to digestive complaints (e.g., diarrhea, bloating, indigestion, etc.) immediately upon ingesting gluten. Severe (or copious) diarrhea happens to be the classic symptom of celiac disease. Sometimes when a patient comes with complaints of severe diarrhea, it is almost as if they have a sign on them that says, "I am a celiac patient".

However, severe diarrhea is not the most common reaction to gluten. Remember, estimates are that nearly 97 percent of those with celiac disease are not being properly diagnosed. The reason they are not being properly diagnosed is that most patients with gluten sensitivity are not having copious diarrhea. These patients have a myriad of symptoms, as listed in Table 3 (Chapter 2, p. 35). Sometimes patients have no symptoms of gluten sensitivity until a critical mass is reached. Researchers have reported that "less than half the patients diagnosed with celiac disease present with diarrhea".[1]

Final Thoughts

This chapter explored some of the consequences of ingesting gluten in those that are sensitive to it. Since gluten sensitivities are so prevalent, we feel anyone suffering from an autoimmune disorder or any of the illnesses listed in Table 4, page 44, should have a therapeutic trial of being gluten-free. A minimum of six weeks is a fair trial to see how you feel off of gluten. If you see an improved health status, then it is wise to remain gluten-free. If you adhere to the diet and see no change in your health, it is unlikely gluten sensitivity is causing a problem.

[1] Cell. Mol. Sci. 2005. Apr;62(7-8):791-9

4

Gluten, The Thyroid, and Autoimmune Disorders

Introduction

As previously stated, gluten sensitivity is woefully under diagnosed; estimates are that 97-99 percent of patients are not being diagnosed. Conventional medicine generally searches for gluten illness only when there is copious diarrhea present. Furthermore, conventional medicine only recognizes this diagnosis if there is damage to the villi of the small intestine, as seen on a biopsy. Gluten sensitivity illnesses are much more common than this, and, in fact, may be affecting millions of people without their knowledge.

Which people are these? These are the patients diagnosed with thyroid or other autoimmune disorders. There are 14 to 23 million Americans (5-8 percent of the U.S. population) presently diagnosed with an autoimmune disorder.[1]

This chapter discusses why patients diagnosed with an autoimmune disorder should be checked for gluten sensitivity, and should therapeutically try a six-week, gluten-free diet to see if their symptoms improve.

Frequently Asked Questions

What Is An Autoimmune Illness?

An autoimmune illness is when the immune system of the body is producing antibodies against its own tissue(s). Autoimmune illnesses are increasing at near epidemic rates. In fact, the number of people diagnosed with an autoimmune disorder has nearly doubled in the U.S. over the past 10 years. [2]

It is not normal for the body to be producing excess antibodies against itself. Conventional medicine has no answer for why this phenomenon is occurring in growing numbers. If you are suffering from an autoimmune disorder, the immune system and probably the digestive system are not working correctly. Approximately 60 percent of our immune system cells are actually located in our gut. So, if there is a gut problem occurring, with the concentration of the immune system in the gut, you can assume the immune system will react to the problem. Oftentimes, immune and, eventually, autoimmune issues can ensue.

How Are Autoimmune Diseases Treated?

Unfortunately, the conventional medical approach to treating autoimmune diseases leaves much to be desired. The conventional approach primarily relies on the use of medications that treat the symptoms of autoimmune illnesses, such as steroids and chemotherapy regimens. Autoimmune disorders do not form from a lack of steroid medications or chemotherapy drugs. There is little research looking at the root causes for autoimmune disorders.

Is Gluten Sensitivity Correlated With Autoimmune Disease?

Gluten sensitivities are certainly one of the underlying causes of many autoimmune disorders. We have seen countless patients with varying autoimmune disorders significantly improve or cure their autoimmune illness by making changes in their diets that include going gluten-free and sometimes also dairy-free.

Another change in the diet that can help all conditions is to avoid refined foods. For more information on ways to improve your diet, we refer the reader to *The Guide to Healthy Eating*.

What Are Autoimmune Thyroid Illnesses?

Hashimoto's and Graves' diseases are the most common autoimmune thyroid problems. Both of these illnesses have been increasing at near epidemic levels over the last 50 years. These illnesses are very difficult to treat if there is a gluten sensitivity issue present. In fact, nearly every patient with an autoimmune disorder (including Graves' and Hashimoto's disease) improves their condition by cleaning up their diet and becoming gluten-free. Just having a gluten sensitivity problem increases the risk of developing thyroid illness.

Researchers have found that there is a 300 percent increased risk of developing thyroid disease in those with celiac disease.[3]

Is Gluten Sensitivity Correlated With Thyroid Autoimmune Illnesses?

It has been well known that celiac disease (i.e., gluten sensitivity) has been associated with a variety of autoimmune illnesses. Research has shown that autoimmune thyroid disease is the second most prevalent autoimmune illness associated with celiac disease after diabetes (Type I).[4] One study found 43 percent of celiac disease patients also have thyroid involvement.[5]

Autoimmune illnesses are much more prevalent in females as compared to males at approximately a 10:1 ratio. Thyroid disorders are more prevalent in females as compared to males in a similar ratio. In fact, thyroid autoimmune diseases are the most frequent autoimmune diseases in the population. They affect approximately 7-8 percent of the population, which encompasses nearly 25 million Americans.[6]

Researchers have suggested that, "As both celiac disease and thyroid diseases have a female preponderance, we should call attention to the importance of screening when a female patient presents {with} one of these diseases."[7] We agree that every patient with an autoimmune thyroid disorder (Graves' or Hashimoto's disease) should be screened for gluten sensitivity. If their illness is very severe or difficult to control, then a therapeutic trial of a gluten-free diet is warranted.

So, What Comes First: Gluten Sensitivity Or Thyroid Illness?

The answer to the above question is not easy to come by. It is the old "chicken or egg" debate. Human beings (and earlier ancestors) have been ingesting meats, fish, fruits, and vegetables for nearly 2 million years. It is only during the last 12,000 years that grains were domesticated for mass consumption. Perhaps we have not yet developed (or evolved) adequate measures to properly digest these grains. In addition, the hybridization and chemical alteration that has taken place over the years add to the changes in nutritional value and digestibility issues. Maladaptation issues would explain the widespread problem humans have with gluten and the rapid rise of autoimmune disorders associated with grain (i.e., gluten) ingestion. Either way, we feel it is best to have a therapeutic trial of becoming gluten-free if you suffer from any thyroid illness, particularly an autoimmune thyroid illness.

What Is The Response Of Thyroid Autoimmune Disorders With A Gluten-Free Diet?

If gluten sensitivity were the underlying cause for developing autoimmune thyroid disorders, it would be logical to suppose that autoimmune thyroid disorders will be resolved with a gluten-free diet. There are reports in medical literature that support this hypothesis. Researchers looked at those patients who had a thyroid disorder as well as celiac disease, and their response to being on a gluten-free diet.[8] Their results were astounding. Hypothyroidism normalized in 71 percent of those studied. Autoimmune thyroid disease normalized in 19 percent of the patients. Furthermore, 60 percent of those with autoimmune thyroid disease significantly improved their illness. Finally, in four of five subjects who had no improvement in thyroid function, the authors comment, "there was poor compliance to the diet".[9]

How Does The Immune System React To Gluten?

The immune system is always on guard for foreign substances. When the body detects a foreign substance that should not be there, it produces antibodies to bind to the foreign substance and neutralize it. This is a normal response by the immune system to keep our bodies healthy. Different parts of the immune system react at different times. You can have an immediate response or a delayed response. An immediate response can occur within minutes of exposure. A delayed response can take up to 72 hours for the response to become apparent.

An immediate response is a reaction such as copious diarrhea happening whenever gluten is ingested. This is an immediate type of an allergic reaction. In this case, gluten may be a direct irritant to the lining of the digestive tract.

Gluten sensitivity can also produce reactions hours or even days after an exposure to gluten. This delayed immune system response is common with the substance gluten, and is one of the reasons why gluten sensitivities are often missed by physicians. It is much harder for a patient or physician to correlate if a symptom expressed is related to an exposure by a substance such as gluten 72 hours previously.

Can Gluten Sensitivity Result In A Leaky Gut?

Yes, this is a third way that gluten can adversely affect the body. If gluten causes enough damage and irritation to the lining of the intestine, it can result in a leaky gut. When you eat food, the digestion process breaks food down into smaller particles such as vitamins and minerals. When things are working correctly, the nutrients from food are properly absorbed and transported to the tissues for use. The remainder of the food is dispensed as stool.

However, if there is too much irritation in the gastrointestinal tract, the cells of the intestine start to pull apart or become leaky. This extra space between them may allow food particles that are normally not absorbed to gain access to the blood system. When this happens, the immune system becomes overactive, trying to produce chemicals (antibodies) to bind to these substances. If there is a chronic leaky gut situation occurring, it can result in an overactive immune system that may eventually lead to autoimmune disorders.

I (DB) have seen leaky gut in many of my patients with autoimmune disorders. In fact, it is rare not to find some gastrointestinal involvement with any autoimmune disorder. Similarly, it is nearly impossible to overcome an autoimmune disorder without ensuring a healthy gastrointestinal system. There are specific stool tests that your doctor can order to determine if leaky gut is occurring.

Final Thoughts

Gluten sensitivity is common and woefully under diagnosed. It may be one of the most important pieces to the riddle of why autoimmune disorders are increasing at such a tremendous rate. Just because you do not have diarrhea with the ingestion of gluten does not rule out a gluten sensitivity/celiac problem. We feel a therapeutic trial of becoming gluten-free for at least six weeks is an appropriate regimen for anyone suffering from an autoimmune disorder. If there is no improvement in your health after becoming completely gluten-free for at least six weeks, other avenues need to be investigated. However, if there is improvement, it is best to remain gluten-free.

[1] NIH Progress in Autoimmune Diseases Research. 2005.

[2] NIH. 2005. IBID.

[3] Am.J. Gastroent. 2001. Mar;967(3);751-7

[4] Am. Fam. Phys. 2002 Dec.15:66(12)2259-66

[5] J.Clin. Gastroent.. 2006: Jan:40(1):33-6

[6] Acta. Biomed. 2003: Apr;74(1):9-33

[7] J. Clin. Gastroent.. 2006. Jan:40(1):33-36

[8] Am. J. Gastroent. 2001. Mar;96(3):751-7

[9] Am. J. Gastroent. IBID. Mar;96(3):751-7

5

Gluten and
Bowel Disorders

Introduction

As mentioned in Chapter 3, there are many chronic illnesses associated with gluten sensitivity. Chronic illness is a complex process that can have many inciting events, such as nutritional deficiencies and toxicities. Many times, it is a combination of factors that lead to the onset of illness. Addressing as many of these factors as possible is essential to achieving the best outcome. We recommend a complete holistic approach to treating a chronic illness.

One of the most common complaints heard by doctors involves bowel problems. Complaints of chronic diarrhea, constipation, and abdominal pain are commonplace today. Our experience has clearly shown that nearly every bowel disorder will improve by eating a healthier diet, free of refined foods. Furthermore, a therapeutic trial of eating a gluten-free diet is warranted in nearly every chronic abdominal condition.

Frequently Asked Questions

What Is Irritable Bowel Syndrome?

Irritable bowel syndrome is defined as abdominal pain or discomfort in the abdomen, often relieved by or associated with a bowel movement. IBS patients can suffer with constipation, diarrhea, or a combination of both. Many times, there is bloating of the abdomen, particularly after eating, and there may be mucus in the stool. Irritable bowel syndrome (IBS) is one of the most common reasons that people seek medical care. In fact, up to 15 percent of adults may experience IBS in their lifetime.[1] There is no definitive test for diagnosing IBS. IBS is often diagnosed based on one's symptoms.

There is no drug therapy that is effective for treating IBS. The reason there is no drug therapy is that IBS is not caused from a deficit of drugs. In our experience, IBS is usually caused by eating poor quality foods and by ingesting foods that cause a sensitivity or allergic reaction in the bowel. Furthermore, most patients with IBS have dysbiosis of the bowel, or imbalance of the good and bad bacteria in the gut.

Is Gluten-Sensitivity Associated With Irritable Bowel Syndrome?

Yes, one of the most common food items that causes or exacerbates IBS is gluten. Anyone with a diagnosis of IBS deserves a therapeutic gluten-free dietary trial. Conventional physicians may scoff at this recommendation, since many people with IBS have had intestinal biopsies that fail to show villi atrophy (see Chapter 2, "Celiac Disease"). However, as previously mentioned, you can have gluten sensitivity without villi atrophy in the biopsy. We have clearly found many patients with IBS improve on an allergy elimination diet, and the most common culprits causing or exacerbating this illness are gluten and/or dairy sensitivity.

What Are Crohn's Disease And Ulcerative Colitis?

Crohn's disease and ulcerative colitis are two inflammatory illnesses of the gastrointestinal tract. These can be very serious, life-threatening illnesses and they are occurring with an ever-increasing frequency. Both illnesses have inflammation and bleeding of the gastrointestinal tract as part of their pathology. Also, these illnesses are considered "autoimmune" in nature since the immune system appears to be attacking its own tissue—in this case, the gastrointestinal tract. Crohn's disease and ulcerative colitis are both characterized by an inflammatory condition whereby the body's own white blood cells are causing inflammation of the intestine.

At present, there is no known cause of Crohn's disease or ulcerative colitis. Conventional medicine's approach to these illnesses is to use strong immunosuppressive drugs, such as steroids, to turn off the inflammatory response. The long-term use of these drugs is fraught with serious side effects.

Is Gluten-Sensitivity Associated With Crohn's Disease and Ulcerative Colitis?

Yes, our experience has been clear: gluten sensitivity is correlated with many of those patients suffering from Crohn's disease and ulcerative colitis. We recommend a trial of a gluten-free diet to anyone suffering from these inflammatory bowel conditions.

Anyone diagnosed with Crohn's disease or ulcerative colitis can benefit from eating a healthier diet and from elimination of all refined foods. Furthermore, we have seen many positive results in eliminating gluten from the diet. Gluten is a very difficult substance to properly digest, even in someone with normal bowel function. In one with an inflammatory bowel disorder, the ingestion of gluten can be disastrous, either causing or exacerbating inflammatory bowel disorder symptoms.

Final Thoughts

Chronic bowel disorders are very commonplace today. Conventional medicine has little that is safe and effective to offer a person suffering from these illnesses. Cleaning up the diet and eliminating refined foods, along with a therapeutic trial of removing gluten from the diet, is indicated in anyone suffering from any chronic bowel disorder. For more information, we refer the reader to **The Guide to Healthy Eating.**

[1] JAMA. Vol. 295. No. 8. 2.22.06

6

Transitioning to a Gluten-Free Lifestyle

Introduction

Having a gluten-free lifestyle is something that initially will take a lot of dedication, education, and patience. Although the transition may be overwhelming at first, over time it will become second nature to you and you will recognize which foods are safe and which foods to avoid. Use this chapter to guide you in making choices and in choosing which foods to eat and which foods to avoid. Taking information with you to the store is recommended until you are familiar with your new diet. See the "Gluten-Free Start-Up Shopping Guide", in Appendix B to help you get started in transitioning to a gluten-free lifestyle.

Frequently Asked Questions

How Do I Begin Transitioning To A Gluten-Free Lifestyle?

First of all, it is important to adopt a completely new approach to how you shop and eat. Education is the very first step required for transitioning to a gluten-free lifestyle. It is very important for you to take ownership of your diet. Phone calls to food companies, reading, and attending gluten-free events will all assist you in learning about a whole new lifestyle. Joining a local support group is a good way to begin to make your change and to learn from others who are eating the same type of diet as you are. See Appendix A for organizations and support group resources.

How Do I Find Out Which Products Are Gluten-Free?

Reading labels is of the utmost importance in order to watch out for gluten ingredients. Carrying a list of foods you can eat and foods you should avoid, such as the one in Appendix B, will be very beneficial, at least initially, as you make the transition. Asking a store manager for information or going to the store with a nutritionist or dietician familiar with gluten-free eating and products can be useful.

Most companies have toll-free customer support phone numbers that you can call to find out the source and manufacturing practices for all of the ingredients.

Until you have researched a product to determine if it is gluten-free, we suggest you avoid it. It is usually safer to buy ingredients and prepare items yourself so that you will know the exact preparation procedures and be sure to avoid cross contamination.

How Do The Food Labeling Laws Help Me In My Transition?

The Food Allergen Labeling and Consumer Protection Act is a law requiring manufacturers to identify the eight major food allergens - milk, eggs, fish, crustacean shellfish, tree nuts, peanuts, wheat, and soybeans - which account for 90 percent of food allergies. FALCPA defines a major food allergen as one of those eight foods previously listed or a food ingredient that contains protein derived from one of those foods.

It is important to double check the facility procedures to be sure food items are never exposed to or cross contaminated with an allergenic food item or derivative. Many manufacturers also state on the label if the item was produced in a facility that also produces any of the major food allergens.

Keep in mind, this labeling law does not regulate many prepared foods, such as what you might find at a deli, fair, or even at a restaurant. More information can be found at http://www.cfsan.fda.gov/ if you look under "Specific Topics and Categories".

Why Is Gluten So Hard To Avoid?

Gluten is what gives many items their taste, smooth texture, and perfect consistency. Gluten is a staple ingredient especially in bread making, because it gives the elasticity and extensibility (stretch) to bread dough. Additionally, the gluten helps trap the carbon dioxide in the dough and enables it to rise with less risk of collapsing. Bread is one of the most difficult food items for people to avoid when they are transitioning to a gluten-free lifestyle. Gluten-free bread does not have the consistency that many people prefer. However, there are many gluten-free types of bread to choose from including those made from rice flour, bean flour, coconut flour, or quinoa for example.

What Foods Can I Eat On A Gluten-Free Diet?

Many of the most common foods we eat on a daily basis are gluten-free. The challenge comes when more processed foods are desired, since processed foods are often made with gluten.

Foods that are gluten-free by nature are plain meat, fish, chicken or turkey, legumes, fruits and vegetables, fats and oils, as well as most dairy foods. Preparing foods yourself is the best way to ensure that you are avoiding gluten. See chapter 7 for ideas on eating out and staying gluten-free.

What Gluten-Free Flour Alternatives Are There?

There are many items that can be used in place of gluten-containing grains to make healthy and good tasting foods. Gluten-free flours often work best in combinations such as blending garfava flour, sorghum flour, corn starch, and tapioca flour for instance. Some of the items used for flour are listed in Table 5. The authors advise against the use of unfermented soy and refer the reader to *The Whole Soy Story, by Kaayla T. Daniel, PhD, CCN*, for more information on soy.

Guar gum, xanthan gum, and gelatin are also gluten-free and often used to improve texture because they act as binders. Experimentation in combining various flours and ingredients will be a key in learning to cook gluten-free. However, there are many books, magazines, and internet resources with ideas and recipes to support you. See Appendix A for many organizations and sources for newsletters, recipes, and tips.

Table 5: Alternatives For Gluten Flours

Arrowroot	Montina
Buckwheat	Pea
Corn/maize	Potatoes
Garfava	Rice
Flax	Soy
Lentils	Tapioca
Millet	Teff

Alternatives Containing Higher Protein And Fiber

Amaranth	Quinoa
Beans	Seeds
Nuts	Sorghum

Are There Any Gluten-Free Packaged Foods?

Yes, there are many companies that are providing packaged foods that are completely gluten-free. Many of them will even say "gluten-free" on the package. It is still important to look at the ingredients to be sure and also to look out for other refined items such as hydrogenated oils or high-fructose corn syrup. If you have other allergies (e.g., corn, soy, dairy, nuts, fish, or shellfish) then you will need to look for those as well.

Some of the packaged foods you can find are pretty decent, whereas others have extremely poor ingredients or just taste terrible. We recommend you meet with a nutritionist or join a support group to get more guidance in this area. Of course, shopping and preparing your own foods is definitely the healthiest and safest route to staying gluten-free.

What Foods Should Be Avoided On A Gluten-Free Diet?

The most obvious foods to avoid include those that are specifically wheat, rye, and barley as well as related grains like spelt, triticale, and kamut. Oat is one item that has some controversy around it on whether it is safe to eat. If the oats are guaranteed to be uncontaminated with wheat, they may be safe to eat. We recommend you check with your physician on whether to avoid oats or not.

Being on a gluten-free diet is not just the avoidance of breads and pastas. There are also many foods that may not be obvious gluten sources. Gluten is found hidden in items such as cold cuts, prepared broths and soups, most processed foods, and even in pharmaceuticals. In addition, the gluten in body products is absorbed into our body directly through the skin.

Some of the obvious, potentially gluten-containing items are listed in Table 6 and their ingredients should always be thoroughly checked. Often on the label it will say what common allergens are in the packages, however, this would only include wheat. Gluten-free is not always listed on the label, therefore, the ingredient list will need to be checked thoroughly. If you are unsure if a product contains gluten, then call the manufacturer before ingesting it.

Table 6: Obvious Gluten Sources

Bagels	Malt vinegar
Barley	Matzo meal
Biscuits	Muesli
Bran	Muffins
Bread	Noodles
Cake	Oats, Oatmeal, Oat bran
Cake meal	Pancakes
Cookies	Pasta
Couscous	Pastries
Crackers	Pie
Croutons	Pretzels
Cupcakes	Rye
Doughnuts	Semolina
Durum	Spaghetti
Flour	Spelt
French toast	Toast
Graham crackers	Tortillas
Gluten	Triticale
Kamut	Waffles
Malt syrup, extract	Wheat flour, germ, starch

If A Product Does Not Say Wheat, Rye, Or Barley, Is It Safe?

Not necessarily. Some gluten sources are a little harder to notice, because they are less commonly known. Familiarize yourself with some of these, which are listed in Table 7. Keep in mind there could also be hidden ingredients in items that do not seem to be obvious sources of gluten (See Table 8 for a more detailed list of those items).

Table 7: Some Of The Other Less Obvious Gluten Sources

Alcohol
Barbeque sauce
Beer
Bulgur
Bran
Bread flour
Brewer's yeast
Caramel coloring
Cereal binding
Cheese
Chewing gum
Chocolate
Couscous
Durum
Einkorn
Farina
Farro
French fries
Gliadin

Graham flour
Groats
Ice cream
Ketchup
Lunch meats
Matzo semolina
Mustard
Non-alcoholic beer
Pharmaceuticals
Rice milk or syrup
Sauces
Sausages
Sherbet
Shortening
Soup
Soy milk or sauce
Vitamins
Whole meal flour
Yogurt (also frozen)

What Are Hidden Ingredients?

Some items contain hidden ingredients that do not obviously come from a gluten source or derivative. These ingredients may have been made on a conveyor belt that was contaminated with wheat flour, or wheat flour may have been used as an anti-caking agent. It is important to avoid foods with ingredients with broad terms such as "spices" or "flavorings" unless you research them. Hidden ingredients are often the additives found in processed foods such as candy, dressings, sauces, seasonings, and soups, as well as in pharmaceuticals and vitamins. See Table 8 for some common additives that may be hidden sources of gluten.

Table 8: Common Additives That May Be Hidden Sources of Gluten

Bouillon	Maltose
Caramel coloring	Modified food starch
Coloring	Mono and diglycerides
Dextrin	MSG
Emulsifiers	Natural flavorings
Fillers	Seasoning
Flavor extracts or flavoring	Soy sauce or shoyu
Hydrolyzed plant or vegetable protein (HPP or HVP)	Spice and spice extracts
	Stabilizers
	Starch
Maltodextrin	Textured vegetable protein (TVP)

Does Wheat Free Mean Gluten-Free?

No, wheat free does not mean that the item is gluten-free. Therefore, being gluten-free is not as simple as just being "wheat free" because gluten is found in many other grains besides wheat, as listed in Table 1 (Chapter 1, p. 20). To become truly gluten-free, you must avoid all grains that contain gluten, including spelt, triticale, kamut, rye, barley, and usually oats. These grains are found in a wide variety of products, including most cereals, pastas, and bread products. You may be getting discouraged thinking there is little to eat that does not contain gluten. However, in chapters to come, you will find many tips, suggestions, and recipes to help you in your transition.

Is Alcohol Gluten-Free?

Yes, some alcohol, such as gin, whiskey, and vodka are safe because the gluten does not remain after distillation. Wines are also usually safe as well. Items to avoid include beer (unless it is gluten-free), ale, and lager.

Can I Eat Sprouted Forms Of Gluten?

The seriousness of your condition will determine whether gluten can be eaten in any form, including sprouted. Sprouting does, in fact, start to break down the gluten in grains; however, it is often not completely broken down and can have remaining hindrances for those intolerant to gluten. It is important to check with your doctor before introducing even sprouted gluten into your diet.

Can I Eat Healthy AND Gluten-Free?

Yes, it is possible to eat healthy AND eat gluten-free. However, it is important to remember that "gluten-free" on the label does not mean the item is "healthy." Many of the common replacement items that are labeled gluten-free can actually cause even more health issues. Many packaged gluten-free items contain refined sugar as the first ingredient, not to mention ingredients such as high fructose corn syrup and other corn derivatives, soy flour and soy oil, and hydrogenated oils as some of the most common ingredients found in gluten-free items. Remember, since you are eliminating many foods in your diet, you want to make sure you are still getting foods with nutrition. Eating a variety of fruits and vegetables or foods high in vitamins and minerals is a priority for a healthy gluten-free diet, or any diet for that matter!

Final Thoughts

Becoming gluten-free is not easy. However, it can be done. It may take a little leg-work on your part, but the end results are worth it. There are hundreds of thousands of people eating a healthy gluten-free diet. Be sure to educate yourself on gluten-free eating so you can implement a gluten-free lifestyle in your household. Use the celiac and gluten-free resources found in Appendix A, as well as the "Gluten-Free Start-Up Shopping Guide" in Appendix B.

7

Eating Out
and Staying
Gluten-Free

Introduction

Many people transitioning to a gluten-free diet are afraid they will never be able to eat out again or go to friends' houses. However, with a little careful planning it is possible to maintain a social life and stay gluten-free. Calling restaurants or host/hostesses before arriving is of utmost importance. See the "Restaurant Guide", in Appendix C to help guide you when eating out. Plan ahead. Bring items with you that you can eat if necessary. When in doubt if something is gluten-free when away from home, it is always safer to just go without. If you always have snacks with you, then you will never go hungry. The three keys to eating out and staying gluten-free are plan ahead, plan ahead, and plan ahead!

Frequently Asked Questions

Can I Still Eat At Restaurants And Be Gluten-Free?

Yes. However, to be safe you will have to prepare ahead of time and be assertive when you arrive at the restaurant. Avoiding fast food or chain restaurants, where food is made out of chemicals or with a lot of additives and fake foods, is a good idea for everyone. Select restaurants where they make your food to order, and call ahead to speak with the chef. By talking to chefs, you can build rapport and inquire whether they can accommodate your gluten-free needs. Work with the chef to explain that your food needs to be prepared separately on clean surfaces, with clean pans, and with clean utensils. Together, see if you can find simple broiled or grilled items that are likely to be safe.

What Steps Should I Take When I Arrive At A Restaurant?

When you arrive at the restaurant, explain to the manager or waitstaff that you have special dietary needs. Make clear that in order for you to avoid becoming ill, particular food preparation is very important. Provide them with a list of foods that are off-limits for you (see the "Restaurant Guide", in Appendix C), so they can understand what you are talking about. Let them know that you have spoken to the chef and then stick to the items you know are safe. Being patient at restaurants is important because most people will not be familiar with gluten-free diet requirements.

What Foods Should I Avoid At A Restaurant?

Any obvious source of gluten should of course be avoided, but there are other precautions to take. Avoid foods that are fried where other problem foods may have been, foods that have sauces, rice or potato dishes that may have been made with a packaged stock containing gluten, salad bars where cross contamination can occur, and intricate dishes with ingredients that are unknown.

Opting for plain broiled or grilled meat or fish and vegetables is usually quite safe if the chef knows to prepare them separately from other meals and problem foods. Do not order any meats or fish that are batter fried or that have breading, spice rubs, marinades, or other possible gluten-containing items.

Simply ask for salt and pepper, or butter, olive oil, herbs, and lemon juice. For a salad, you can use oil and balsamic vinegar or some lemon juice (no croutons, of course!). In fact, look at *The Guide to Healthy Eating*, and prepare your own salad dressing.

Are There Any Restaurants That Cater Specifically To Gluten-Free Diets Or That Have Special Menus?

Yes, there are restaurants that have been found to be better than others when it comes to preparing gluten-free items. Visit www.glutenfreerestaurants.org to find a restaurant in your area. Other resources include books such as *The Essential Gluten-Free Resource Guide*, by Triumph Dining or *Let's Eat Out!: Your Passport to Living Gluten And Allergy Free*, by Kim Koeller and Robert La France. Remember, we are not endorsing the recommendations found online or in other books. Also, these are not guaranteed lists of gluten-free restaurants, due to the fact that every area has different guidelines and, even in a chain, one location can vary from another in their practices and service capabilities.

Asking others about their experiences is the best way to begin creating your own list of safe places to eat. Use the resources listed in Appendix A to find support groups that may be able to give you a good head start.

Can I Still Eat At Friends' Or Relatives' Houses?

Yes, it is important to still be social and enjoy being with friends even if you are gluten-free. Calling your host or hostess ahead of time is a good idea so they can understand what you can and cannot eat. Ask them to leave your salad free of croutons and maybe to pull aside a piece of meat or fish before adding marinade or sauces to it. You can usually expect vegetable, fruit, or cheese platters at a party, but offer to bring a dish to pass so you can ensure that you will have at least one thing to eat!

What Can I Take With Me In Case The Place I Am Going Has Nothing Gluten-Free?

It is always important to have snacks on hand if you are traveling or if you are running late for an event and you get there and find nothing safe to eat. Simply carrying small bags of nuts, seeds, dried fruit, fruit leather, rice crackers, trail mixes, homemade muffins, etc. is a good idea whenever you leave the house. Invest in a small cooler and carry fresh fruits and vegetables, yogurt, cheese or meat slices, nut butters or hummus. Have snacks pre-packed so you can just grab them as you walk out the door. Also, keep some stashed at the office, in your purse, and other places you frequent.

Can I Still Travel Out Of Town And Eat Gluten-Free?

Yes, it is possible to travel. Carry snacks with you. Also, avoiding fast food is probably a good idea, since that is often a source of gluten-containing additives and packaged foods. Calling ahead to the hotel concierge or working with a good travel agent may be worthwhile to ensure a good experience.

What Are Some Resources For Eating Out And Traveling Gluten-Free?

A gluten-free dining and travel club can be found at http://bobandruths.com. Another website to help you plan your vacation and ensure gluten-free meals on flights and throughout your trip is http://www.glutenfreeholidays.com.

Final Thoughts

Gluten-free dining and eating away from home may seem overwhelming at first. However, with guides such as the one in Appendix C, you will soon feel comfortable eating out. Planning ahead and always having safe food on hand is extremely important. As more and more people become aware of the problems of gluten, maintaining a gluten-free lifestyle will continue to get easier.

8

Children and a Gluten-Free Lifestyle

Introduction

If your child was recently diagnosed with celiac disease or gluten sensitivity, then it is important for you to become as educated as possible to support your child. This chapter will offer you ways to prepare yourself and your child for living a gluten-free lifestyle. It is imperative for children to be included in the learning process and in what it means to be on a gluten-free diet. Give your child lots of support and guidance so that as they grow older they will be able to make proper and safe selections when they are away from home and your supervision.

Frequently Asked Questions

If One Child In A Family Has To Be Gluten-Free, Should The Whole Family Become Gluten-Free?

Yes and no. It is very important to support the emotional and physical well-being of a child by letting them know they are not alone and, of course, by making sure they do not get sick from eating foods they should not. Most of the time, it would be ideal for a whole family to eat gluten-free so the child does not feel left out, abnormal, or unhappy at meal or snack times. This also maintains safety by avoiding cross contamination. In the home, it is best for the whole family to be gluten-free. Some people are so sensitive that they cannot even have a crumb of gluten contaminating their food. However, eating out at restaurants would be a different story. Perhaps the rest of the family could eat as they choose at a restaurant. Every family finds their own balance and comfort level in this area. Keep in mind that, while at home, it might not be a good idea to serve one child a gluten item while the other is given a gluten-free item and made to feel like they are missing out.

Should We Get Rid Of All Gluten Foods In Our Home To Protect Our Children From Exposure?

This is not always completely necessary if some of the family is still choosing to eat gluten-containing items. Many precautions would have to be taken. If the children are small enough, the parents will be making all meals and snacks. If they are older, then special cabinets or cooking areas could be designated either off-limits or safe for gluten sensitive children. A certain color code or sign could be used for which foods, utensils, or items are safe and which are not safe. Involving the children in the cooking process is the best way for them to learn what items they can have and which they should avoid.

How Do I Ensure My Child Will Not Be Exposed To Gluten At School?

It is important to meet with your child's teacher prior to the start of school to go over your child's needs. A main area of caution is during lunch and snack time. It is advisable to always send a packed lunch so you do not have to worry about the lunch line and what selections might be contaminated. Also, you will want to plan ahead of time with the teacher to determine what types of snacks will be similar to those of the other children, as well as to plan a few special snacks in case there is a birthday treat.

Many schools now have separate eating areas at lunchtime for children with various allergies, so they can eat with other children that are avoiding the same foods. In addition, projects such as play-doh, clays, pasta art, pastes, and papier mache can be risks of exposure, as gluten is contained in many items.

What Are Some Steps I Can Take Before My Child Goes To Events Away From Home?

Always prepare in advance for school lunches, parties, play dates, games, camps, etc. to be sure you have food packed for your child. Call ahead and find out what is being served and try to have something similar for your child to eat so he/she will not feel left out. You may even look into camps specifically for children with celiac disease or food allergies so your child can enjoy all the food with the rest of the campers. Be sure to make all friends, parents, relatives, coaches, and teachers aware of your child's specific needs and what to do in case of an emergency.

How Can I Prepare My Children For An Event Away From Home?

Educate your children about what you are trying to accomplish. We know this is not easy for anyone, much less a child. But, once they feel better, most children are more than willing to go the extra mile. Giving them a list of safe foods and foods to avoid will help them be more confident when traveling (see Appendix B). Remind them to ask an adult before eating anything to be sure it is free of gluten or whatever items they are to avoid. Another option is to go with your children and help them determine which foods are safe to eat before leaving them. You can even send some safe snacks along just in case there is nothing suitable to eat. Leave your phone number so you can be contacted if there is uncertainty about any foods. Better to be safe than sorry!

How Can I Teach My Child About Why Eating Gluten-free Is Important?

As soon as your children are old enough, be sure to educate them about their condition and the necessity of eating the foods you have packed or foods that are permitted wherever they are. Make sure they know how imperative it is to their health that they stick to their diet. Explain the ramifications of eating foods that are off-limits and why it might make them feel very sick. You may read them stories about children who need to avoid gluten such as *Eating Gluten-Free with Emily* by Bonnie J. Kruszka. Also, take them to resources online such as www.clubceliac.com or other kid-friendly, gluten-free resources. Children need to realize they are not alone in eating a gluten-free diet.

How Do I Get My Children To Be Responsible For Their Own Health And The Food They Eat?

Younger children can learn more by being involved in the kitchen and the preparation of foods. Including them in the mixing, pouring, and serving can build their confidence. Children love to help and they love to have fun – so let them do both while making foods they can enjoy safely on their gluten-free diet. Older children can help by reading labels at the grocery store and meal planning, as well as in the preparation of meals and snacks.

Final Thoughts

One of the most important things to remember with children and a gluten-free diet is to include them in the process. Educating them about their diet and involving them in the shopping, preparing, and cooking will help them with their confidence and self-esteem.

Recommended Books

Eating Gluten-Free with Emily, Bonnie J. Kruszka

Gluten-Free Friends, An Activity Book for Kids, by Nancy Patin Falini, MA, RD, LDN

Incredible Edible Gluten–Free Food for Kids, Sheri L. Sanderson

Kids with Celiac Disease, Danna Korn who founded Raising Our Celiac Kids (R.O.C.K.), a support group for families of children with celiac disease.

The GF Kid, by Melissa London and Eric Glickman

9

Cooking and Preparing Gluten-Free

Introduction

Cooking and preparing gluten-free will become second nature to you with a little practice. The following chapter will give you some shopping ideas and also some tips to avoid cross contamination. Creating a safe kitchen is important to ensure items are completely gluten-free. Many cooking utensils and appliances will have to be strictly for gluten-free cooking and preparation. Furthermore, be sure to join a local support group and check online resources, such as those listed in Appendix A. Others who have been living gluten-free will have many suggestions, tips, and ideas to give you a good head start in the preparation of gluten-free items.

Frequently Asked Questions

Are There Any Gluten-Free Stores?

Yes, there are more and more gluten-free stores popping up since celiac disease and gluten sensitivity are much more prevalent. There are also many gluten-free stores online that can ship products directly to your home. Your local health food store will most likely have a good selection of gluten-free items. Moreover, many grocery stores are now beginning to include several gluten-free choices in their aisles or in their bakeries, which is making it even easier to find gluten-free selections. Use the "Gluten-Free Start-Up Shopping Guide", in Appendix B, to help guide you when shopping.

How Do I Avoid Cross Contamination When Shopping Gluten-free?

First of all, you want to buy food from sources you trust. Do not buy foods from bulk bins where containers and scoops are often shared amongst other products that may have wheat. Ask workers at deli and prepared food counters to clean their gloves, the working area, the slicer, serving utensils, or knives before making your portion. Be sure to look for foods made in facilities where they do not process gluten products, or at least have strict procedures to avoid cross contamination.

Read and re-read labels often to be sure the ingredient list or the processing techniques have not been changed. Common prepared foods such as stocks and soups, yogurt, ice cream, snack foods, and processed meats (e.g., lunch meats and sausages) may have gluten ingredients. Unsuspected foods would be items such as licorice, soy sauce, and flavorings.

What Other Items Might I Shop For Regularly That May Contain Gluten?

Common items such as postage stamps and envelope adhesive may have gluten in them, so you do not want to lick them. Play-doh, clays, and paints may have gluten in them, therefore, you need to either avoid them or wear gloves if using these items. Shampoos, toothpastes, lotions, and other toiletries could have gluten or could have been made using flour during production, so these items need to be chosen carefully. Drugs and vitamins commonly contain gluten and must be checked by asking your pharmacist for the exact ingredients to be sure there is no gluten.

How Can I Get More Nutrition In A Gluten-Free Diet?

There are many ways to add more nutrition, including some fiber, to a gluten-free diet. Using brown rice instead of white rice flour in recipes, using beans in your salads, and eating a variety of fruits and vegetables every day can help. In addition, adding chopped dried fruits, nuts, and seeds to yogurt or salad can add more flavor and variety to your diet. Snack ideas include items such as popcorn, trail mixes, fruit, raw veggies, and dips like hummus, salsa, or guacamole. Many more meal and snack ideas, as well as various recipes can be found in Chapter 10.

How Do I Keep My Kitchen Safe For Cooking Gluten-free?

This seems easy when you first think about it, but then you need to realize that the toaster, grill, cutting boards, knives, counters, pans, etc. can all be contaminated with gluten. Separate items, as well as separate cooking areas, should be set up. Washing hands before cooking becomes of the utmost importance. Gluten-containing flour can stay in the air for several hours after baking, so it may contaminate cooking areas and foods you are planning to prepare gluten-free. Often, cooking the gluten-free meal first allows you to reuse utensils and items that can be used for both types of meals and allows you to put away the gluten-free items so they do not become contaminated. Also, condiments and shared containers (e.g., mustard, mayonnaise, jams, peanut butters, spreads, etc.) can be an area of cross contamination and should be purchased separately to ensure they are kept gluten-free.

Are There Any Tips For Baking Gluten-Free Foods?

Yes, often baking gluten-free items requires some alteration to the recipe and the preparation. We suggest you experiment with some recipes from books before trying your own concoctions. To get different textures when baking, you may vary the flour blends as you desire. See Chapter 10 for several basic recipes to get you started.

Gluten-free breads are difficult to get to the right texture and are always best the first day warm, or on later days when toasted. Moreover, many baked goods requiring a flour of some sort need something that will bind them together as gluten would. Examples of binders you can buy at the grocery store that work well for gluten-free baking are eggs, xanthan gum, guar gum, and gelatin. Xanthan gum and guar gum also prevent crumbling in baked goods, whereas, eggs will be useful both as a binder and to help baked goods rise (or leaven).

Investing in a small coffee grinder will come in handy to grind up various flours, nuts, or seeds for recipes you are making. You can also grind up rice, flax, or quinoa for baking.

Final Thoughts

Gluten-free baking will seem daunting at first. However, it can be done. It takes a little work on your part, but the rewards are more than worth it. Do not worry about making mistakes, just learn from them. Sharing ideas with others living a gluten-free lifestyle is a great way to shorten your learning curve. Within a short period of time, your confidence will increase and you will become more and more successful with your gluten-free cooking and baking.

10

Gluten-Free Meal Ideas, Tips, and Recipes

Introduction

Becoming gluten-free does not mean you have to give up all of your favorite foods. However, what it does mean is that you will have to alter your meals and recipes to gluten-free ingredients and prepare them to avoid cross contamination with gluten containing items. Experimentation will be the key to finding what works best for you and your family. Use the following meal ideas, tips, and recipes to guide you as you are learning about a gluten-free lifestyle.

Meal Ideas

The following are some ideas for meals that are safe to eat on a gluten-free diet. You will soon be able to come up with your own favorites and make changes and alterations to fit your tastes and desires.

Breakfast

- ❖ Gluten-free warm cereals (e.g., cream of rice, cream of buckwheat) with cinnamon, coconut oil, butter, sea salt, raw honey, fruit, yogurt

- ❖ Gluten-free toast with butter, coconut oil, jam, nut butters, cream cheese

- ❖ Gluten-free waffles or pancakes with butter, jam, fresh strawberries or blueberries, maple syrup

- ❖ Egg sandwich on gluten-free toast with cream cheese, sliced tomato, sea salt

- ❖ Egg omelet with various vegetables (eg., spinach, tomato, peppers, onion, cheese)

- ❖ Fruit smoothies with gluten-free yogurt or coconut milk and various berries or fruits, raw honey, nut butter, flax

- ❖ Gluten-free yogurt with nuts, seeds, berries

- ❖ Gluten-free muffins topped with butter or nut butter

- ❖ Gluten-free turkey sausage

Lunch or Dinner

- ❖ Gluten-free soups (e.g., chicken and rice, lentil, split pea, vegetable, bean, chili)

- ❖ Gluten-free bread, toasted and topped with melted cheese (grilled cheese)

- ❖ Gluten-free bread, toasted and topped with melted cheese and tomato or gluten-free tomato sauce (mini-pizza)

- ❖ Gluten-free tortilla with vegetables, meats, beans, cheese or other items to make a wrap or quesadilla

- ❖ Gluten-free pasta with gluten-free spaghetti sauce

- ❖ Gluten-free salad with various vegetables, beans, meat, fish, egg, cheese, and gluten-free salad dressing (hold the croutons, of course!)

- ❖ Gluten-free stir-fry with vegetables, brown rice, wild rice, or quinoa

- ❖ Gluten-free chili or stew

- ❖ Gluten-free taco salad with lettuce, meat, salsa, sour cream, cheese, and gluten-free corn chips

- ❖ Gluten-free stuffed peppers or stuffed cabbage with meat, vegetables, rice, or quinoa

- ❖ Gluten-free meatballs or meatloaf using brown rice breadcrumbs

- ❖ Gluten-free turkey or chicken rubbed with butter, sea salt, herbs, pepper, and roasted in the oven

- ❖ Gluten-free grilled salmon or other fish and a vegetable side

❖ Gluten-free grilled hamburger patty, steak, or chicken breast with herbs or sea salt and a side of steamed vegetables

❖ Gluten-free meatloaf with finely chopped vegetables such as carrots, zucchini, onions, spinach, red peppers, etc.

Snacks

❖ Fresh fruit – plain or with a yogurt fruit dip

❖ Popcorn with coconut oil, butter, sea salt, nutritional yeast

❖ Dried fruits

❖ Nuts and nut mixes

❖ Pumpkin and sunflower seeds

❖ Vegetables and dips

❖ Rice crackers and hummus, nut butters, cheese

❖ Gluten-free crackers or bread and artichoke spinach dip

❖ Deviled eggs

❖ Corn chips and salsa

❖ Cheese slices

❖ Yogurt and fruit, nuts, seeds

- ❖ Fruit smoothies with coconut milk or yogurt

- ❖ Gluten-free bread and nut butter

- ❖ Gluten-free muffins

- ❖ Celery, apples, pears, or bananas with almond or other nut butters

- ❖ Gluten-free cookies

- ❖ Sherbet

- ❖ Sweet potatoes

- ❖ Olives

- ❖ Store bought gluten-free snacks (many companies have gluten-free offerings, be sure to check ingredient list first!)

General Gluten-Free Tips

The following tips will assist you in your gluten-free transitioning. You may find you have to try a recipe several times before you are satisfied with the results. Over time, you will become more familiar with substitutes and alternatives to make baking and preparing gluten-free items simple.

- ❖ Bread needs to be sliced and frozen immediately upon making or buying it. Separate slices with waxed paper for easy removal.

- ❖ Bread tastes better fresh out of the oven, slightly warmed, or toasted.

- ❖ Leftover gluten-free bread can make great bread crumbs for meatloaf, meatballs, or other dishes

- ❖ Look online for gluten-free toaster bags if there are people in your household using the toaster for gluten containing items (www.allergygrocer.com)

- ❖ Buy liners for bakeware, ovens, frying pans, and microwaves to avoid cross-contamination (www.allergygrocer.com)

- ❖ Get more fiber in your diet by adding beans to salads and meals and eating a variety of fruits and vegetables daily

- ❖ Add flavor to salads and meals by adding chopped nuts, seeds, and dried fruits

- ❖ Experiment with alternative starches such as brown rice or corn tortillas, corn chips, quinoa or brown rice pastas, rices, quinoa, millet, amaranth, and potatoes.

- ❖ Ground nuts make great flours, pie crusts, dessert toppings

- ❖ Hide vegetables in sauces, cookies, muffins, hamburgers, meatloaf, or meatballs to add nutritional value

- ❖ Potato, corn and arrowroot starches tend to add lightness to baked goods

- ❖ Bean and nut flours add more protein and fiber to your recipes

- ❖ Xanthan and guar gums help prevent crumbling in your recipes

- ❖ Combinations of flours work best for gluten-free baking (see recipes to follow and other cookbooks for examples and ideas on which flours to use)

- ❖ Gluten-free flours require some sort of binder to bake properly (e.g., xanthan gum, guar gum, eggs, gelatin)

- ❖ Make flour blends ahead of time and store them in the freezer for easy baking use

- ❖ Yeast, eggs, baking powder, and baking soda are all used to help leaven baked goods (i.e., help them rise)

- ❖ Refrigerate gluten-free baked goods to decrease crumbling

Recipes

These recipes are meant to give you a basic start for your gluten-free lifestyle. Many of the recipes are kid-friendly, too! Please refer to the authors' other book called **The Guide to Healthy Eating** for many more recipes that can easily be made gluten-free. Although you can find many pre-made and packaged items at a variety of stores, we encourage you to prepare as many items as you can at home. Remember, baking and cooking gluten-free may take extra effort, practice, and especially patience in the beginning, but pretty soon will become second-nature to you.

NOTE: When purchasing the ingredients to make the following recipes, the authors are assuming you are buying gluten-free versions of each listed ingredient.

Breakfast Recipes

- ❖ Spice Muffins (Variations - with apple, blueberry, carrot and raisins)
- ❖ Cinnamon Waffles
- ❖ Egg Sandwich

Lunch Recipes

- ❖ Cheesy Macaroni Dish
- ❖ Chicken Fingers
- ❖ Ginger Quinoa Squash
- ❖ Taco Salad

Dinner Recipes

- ❖ Chicken Quinoa
- ❖ Sloppy Lentils
- ❖ Spaghetti (Variation - Chicken Parmesan)
- ❖ Vegetable Rice Stir-Fry

Dip Recipes

- ❖ Yogurt Fruit Dip
- ❖ Yogurt Ranch Dip

Cookie Recipes

- ❖ Banana Cookies
- ❖ Chocolate Chip Cookies

Dessert Recipes

- ❖ Apple Crisp
- ❖ Applesauce Cake
- ❖ Brown Rice Crispy Snacks
- ❖ Delicious Brownie Cake
- ❖ Chocolate-Fudgy Frosting

Spice Muffins

2	cups brown rice flour
1½	cups whole, plain yogurt
2	teaspoons baking soda
1	teaspoon cinnamon
½	teaspoon xanthan gum
½	teaspoon sea salt
¼	teaspoon ground ginger
¼	teaspoon ground cloves
⅔	cup coconut oil, melted
⅔	cup Sucanat
2	free-range eggs
1	teaspoon vanilla

Servings: 22-24

Prep: 10 minutes   Cook: 18 minutes

Combine flour and yogurt in a large bowl and let soak overnight. Add baking soda, all spices, and xanthan gum to yogurt mixture and set aside. In a separate bowl, blend oil with Sucanat. Add eggs, vanilla, and optional fruit, carrot, or raisins (see below) and mix. Slowly add yogurt mixture to carrot mixture and stir until moistened. Fill muffin cups in a muffin pan and bake at 300°F for about 20 minutes,

Variations (baking time may vary)

Apple Spice Muffins – Add ½ - ¾ cup diced apples

Blueberry Spice Muffins – Add ½ - ¾ cup blueberries

Carrot Spice Muffins – Add ¼ - ½ cup grated carrots

Raisin Spice Muffins – Add ½ - ¾ cup raisins

Cinnamon Waffles

1	cup brown rice flour
½	cup coconut flour
1⅔	cups whole, plain yogurt
1	tablespoon butter, melted
1	tablespoon agave nectar or maple syrup
3	free-range eggs
½	cup arrowroot starch
1	teaspoon baking soda
1	teaspoon sea salt
1½	teaspoons cinnamon
¼	teaspoon xanthan gum
1-2	tablespoons sparkling water (to desired consistency)

Servings: 6-8

Prep: 10 minutes   Cook: 15 minutes

Combine flours with yogurt and let soak overnight. The next day, blend butter and agave or maple syrup together. Add eggs and mix. Add arrowroot, baking soda, sea salt, cinnamon, xanthan gum, and the flour/yogurt mixture and mix until well blended. Add sparkling water to thin the waffle mix, as necessary. Pour by spoonfuls onto waffle maker and heat through. Top with butter, maple syrup, or fruit and enjoy!

Egg Sandwich

2	teaspoons coconut oil
1	free-range egg
1	piece gluten-free bread
1	tablespoon butter
1	tablespoon cream cheese (optional)
1	pinch sea salt

Servings: 1

Prep: 5 minutes   *Cook: 8 minutes*

Heat pan over medium heat. Melt coconut oil and crack egg into pan. Cook egg 2-3 minutes until top of white has just begun to set. Flip and cook 1-2 more minutes ("over easy" style egg). While egg is cooking, toast the bread. Spread toasted bread with butter and optional cream cheese. Place cooked egg on top. Sprinkle with sea salt and serve.

Serving Suggestions: *Serve with thinly sliced tomato.*

Cheesy Macaroni Dish

2	cups brown rice elbow pasta
6	tablespoons of butter
1	cup whole, plain yogurt
½	teaspoon onion flakes
¼	teaspoon nutmeg
¼	teaspoon white pepper
¼	teaspoon black pepper
⅛	teaspoon sea salt
2	pinches dried mustard
1	cup chicken broth
¼	cup arrowroot powder
2	free-range eggs, lightly beaten
2	cups shredded cheese
½	cup Romano cheese, grated

Servings: 8

Prep: 25 minutes   *Cook: 30 minutes*

Preheat oven to 350°F. Cook pasta al dente style or 2 minutes less than time on package, drain and set aside. While pasta is cooking, melt butter in a medium size pan. Add yogurt and spices and bring to slow boil. In small container, combine chicken broth with arrowroot powder and shake. Slowly pour broth mixture into pan with yogurt and continue stirring until it begins to thicken. Lightly beat eggs and add to mixture along with both of the cheeses and stir until melted. Add al dente pasta to cheese mixture until coated. Transfer to a greased 9 X 13 dish and spread evenly. Bake covered at 350°F for 15 minutes, remove cover and bake another 10 minutes or until bubbly all over. Broil 2-3 minutes until the top is lightly browned before serving.

Cheesy Macaroni Dish Variations

- Add gluten-free bread crumbs on top before baking

- Sprinkle paprika and parsley on top before baking.

- Add 2 cups chopped chicken and 1 cup peas to mixture before baking and make a Cheesy Chicken and Macaroni Casserole

- Add 1 pound cooked ground beef and ⅔ cup ketchup to a half recipe of Cheesy Macaroni and you have dinner for one more night!

Chicken Fingers

1	cup gluten-free bread crumbs
2	teaspoons Italian seasoning
2	teaspoons garlic seasoning
1	teaspoon sea salt
1	teaspoon pepper
2	free-range eggs
1	pound chicken cut into strips

Servings: 4

Prep: 10 minutes   Cook: 30 minutes

In one bowl combine bread crumbs and seasonings. In another bowl beat egg. Dip chicken strips into egg to cover and then dip into bread crumb mixture until coated. Place on greased cookie sheet and then bake in oven 20-30 minutes or until cooked through.

Serving Suggestion: Serve with gluten-free honey mustard, teriyaki sauce, or a combination of the two.

Ginger Quinoa Squash

1	butternut squash
½	cup quinoa
¾	cup water
½	teaspoon ginger
1-2	tablespoons organic butter
1	teaspoon raw honey

Servings: 4

Prep: 10 minutes   Cook: 85 minutes

Preheat oven to 300°F. Cut butternut squash in half and remove seeds. Place skin side up into about 1 inch of water in a Pyrex dish and bake at 300°F for about 55 minutes or until tender. While squash is baking, make quinoa by rinsing it and placing it in a saucepan covered with ¾ cup water. Bring water to boil, turn down heat and simmer about 20 minutes or until tender; set aside. Remove cooked squash from skin and mash in a small pan. Stir in ginger and butter and heat over low heat. Add cooked quinoa and top with honey before serving.

Note: Quinoa is easier to digest if you soak it overnight in water and 2 tablespoons lemon juice prior to cooking. Rinse quinoa after soaking. Add to cooking water and cook as recipe describes.

Serving Suggestions: *Serve in the skin from the squash.*

Taco Salad

1	pound free-range, ground turkey (or ground beef)
2	tablespoons tomato paste
1	tablespoon chili powder
1½	teaspoons ground cumin
¼	teaspoon garlic powder
¼	teaspoon onion powder
¼	teaspoon paprika
1	teaspoon sea salt
½	teaspoon black pepper
½	cup broth (or water)

Servings: 4

Prep: 10 minutes   Cook: 25 minutes

Brown the turkey in a skillet over medium-high heat. Drain meat and put back in skillet. Stir in the tomato paste, all of the spices, and the broth. Simmer about 15 minutes, stirring occasionally.

Serving Suggestions: *Serve over lettuce with shredded raw cheese, tomatoes, black olives, black beans, sour cream or yogurt, salsa, guacamole, and crumbled blue corn chips.*

Chicken Quinoa

1	teaspoon sea salt
4	chicken breasts
2	tablespoons coconut oil
½	cup onion, diced
2	cloves garlic, minced
1	cup white wine
½	cup spinach or Swiss chard, chopped
4½ -5	cups chopped tomatoes

Servings: 4-6

Prep: 10 minutes   Cook: 60 minutes

Season the chicken with sea salt. Heat coconut oil over medium-high heat and then brown the chicken on both sides. Set chicken aside. Sauté the onions and garlic until soft. Add chicken and white wine and simmer for 10 minutes. Add spinach or Swiss chard and tomatoes. Simmer for 35-40 minutes. Serve over quinoa (see preparation below). *Optional: Top with chopped black olives and/or parmesan cheese.*

Quinoa Preparation

2	cups quinoa
3	cups filtered water
2	tablespoons butter
1	teaspoon sea salt

While chicken is simmering, rinse the quinoa. Put quinoa in filtered water and bring to a boil. Add butter and sea salt, reduce to simmer and cover for 10-15 minutes or until water is absorbed. *Note: Quinoa is easier to digest if you soak it overnight in water and 2 tablespoons lemon juice prior to cooking. Rinse quinoa after soaking and cook as recipe describes.*

Sloppy Lentils

1½	cups lentils (uncooked)
3	cups filtered water
1	tablespoon lemon juice
½	cup green pepper, chopped
½	cup onion, chopped
3	cups tomatoes, diced
1	tablespoon chili powder
2	teaspoons cumin
1	teaspoon sea salt
2	tablespoons Worcestershire sauce
1	tablespoon Dijon mustard
1	tablespoon maple syrup

Servings: 4-6

Prep: 20-25 minutes   Cook: 5-6 hours

Soak lentils overnight in water with lemon juice. Drain and rinse before placing into a crock pot. Add the rest of the ingredients to the crockpot with the lentils. Cover and cook on high-heat setting for 5-6 hours (or on low-heat setting for 10-12 hours). Lentils should be soft enough to eat.

Serving Suggestions: *Serve with sour cream or yogurt, open face on a piece of gluten-free bread. Top with raw cheese.*

Spaghetti Sauce

1	pound organic ground beef or turkey
2	tablespoons coconut oil
½	cup onion, diced
½	cup green pepper, diced
½	cup red pepper, diced
3	cloves garlic, minced
2	teaspoons Italian seasoning
1	teaspoon sea salt
1	teaspoon oregano
1	teaspoon parsley
¼	teaspoon black pepper
¼	teaspoon marjoram
3	cups tomato sauce
½	cup tomato paste

Servings: 4-6

Prep: 15 minutes   Cook: 30 minutes

Brown meat and set aside. Sauté onions and peppers with all spices in coconut oil until soft. Combine meat, onion/pepper/spice mixture with tomato sauce and tomato paste. Simmer sauce for 20 minutes on lowest heat. Serve over spaghetti squash or brown rice pasta.

Variation – Make spaghetti sauce without meat and make chicken finger recipe on page 133. Spread spaghetti sauce over chicken fingers, top with cheese and broil until cheese is melted to make chicken parmigiana dish.

Vegetable Rice Stir-Fry

¼	cup onion, chopped
½	teaspoon ground ginger
½	teaspoon garlic or 1 clove, chopped
3	tablespoons coconut oil
3	tablespoons water
2	carrots, chopped
1	red pepper, chopped
½	zucchini, chopped
½	head kale, chopped
3	tablespoons gluten-free soy or teriyaki sauce
½	cup raw slivered almonds
1	cup brown or wild rice, cooked

Servings: 2-3

Prep: 25 minutes   *Cook: 15 minutes*

Sauté the onions, ginger, and garlic in coconut oil over medium-high heat for 3-5 minutes or until tender. Add water and the rest of the vegetables and stir-fry in the pan. When vegetables are close to being done add soy or teriyaki sauce and almonds. Stir cooked rice into vegetables and serve.

Yogurt Fruit Dip

1½	cups yogurt
½	cup cream cheese
2	teaspoons vanilla
6	drops vanilla stevia or ½ tablespoon maple syrup

Place ingredients in a food processor and blend until smooth. Refrigerate before serving. Serve with fresh strawberries, grapes, pineapple, apples, or other fruit you enjoy.

Yogurt Ranch Dip

1	cup strained yogurt (or use sour cream)
1	teaspoon dill
½	teaspoon onion powder
½	teaspoon garlic powder
½	teaspoon parsley

sea salt and pepper to taste

Mix ingredients until well blended, adjust seasonings to taste. Refrigerate before serving. Serve with fresh chopped carrots, celery, bell peppers, broccoli, cucumbers, or other vegetables you enjoy.

Banana Cookies

1	cup coconut flour
½	cup arrowroot starch
1	teaspoon baking soda
½	teaspoon sea salt
¼	teaspoon xanthan gum
¼	teaspoon cinnamon
1	cup Sucanat
5	tablespoons butter
3	free-range eggs
1	banana, mashed

Servings: 20

Prep: 25 minutes   Cook: 15 minutes

Preheat oven to 350 degrees. Combine dry ingredients and set aside. In large mixing bowl mix Sucanat and butter together until creamy. Add eggs and mashed banana and mix well. Slowly add dry ingredients and mix completely. Place by spoonfuls on a greased cookie sheet and press down slightly to flatten a bit. Bake for 10-12 minutes and serve!

Variation – Add ½ cup gluten-free chocolate chips (omit the cinnamon).

Chocolate Chip Cookies

¾	cup coconut flour
½	cup arrowroot flour
¼	teaspoon guar gum
¼	teaspoon sea salt
6	tablespoons butter
¾	cup Sucanat
3	free-range eggs
1	teaspoon vanilla
1	cup chocolate chips

Servings: 20

Prep: 25 minutes   *Cook: 15 minutes*

Preheat oven to 350 degrees. Combine flours, guar gum, and sea salt and set aside. Blend butter and Sucanat. Add eggs and vanilla and mix. Combine with flour mixture. Stir in chocolate chips. Place in rounded spoonfuls on a greased cookie sheet and press down slightly to flatten a bit. Bake for 15 minutes and serve.

Apple Crisp

5-6	apples, peeled, cored, sliced
2	tablespoons lemon juice
½	cup Sucanat
½	cup coconut flour
½	cup pecans
¾	teaspoon cinnamon
¼	teaspoon sea salt
8	tablespoons butter (1 stick), firm

Servings: 6-8

Prep: 20 minutes   Cook: 25-30 minutes

Preheat oven to 375 degrees. Combine apples and lemon juice to keep apples from browning and place in a buttered 8 X 8 pyrex dish. In food processor, blend Sucanat and other ingredients (except butter). Add butter and pulse until combined, but still crumbly. Sprinkle mixture over apples until covered. Bake 25-30 minutes or until browned and bubbling.

Applesauce Cake

1	cup brown rice flour
1	teaspoon baking soda
½	teaspoon baking powder
½	teaspoon cinnamon
½	teaspoon cloves
½	cup coconut oil
1	cup Sucanat
1	free-range egg
1	cup applesauce
½	cup raisins or zante currants (optional)

Servings: 6-8

Prep: 15 minutes   Cook: 35 minutes

Preheat oven to 300°F. In a small bowl, mix brown rice flour, baking soda, baking powder, cinnamon, and cloves; set aside. In a large mixing bowl mix coconut oil and Sucanat together until creamy and then add egg and applesauce. Slowly pour the flour mixture into the applesauce mixture and mix completely. Stir the raisins or currants in by hand. Bake in a well greased 8 X 8 inch Pyrex dish (try using coconut oil) at 300°F for approximately 35 minutes.

Serving Suggestions: *Serve with applesauce.*

Brown Rice Crispy Snacks

1 cup brown rice syrup
½ cup raw almond butter or other nut butter
½ cup gluten-free chocolate chips
3 cups crispy brown rice cereal

Servings: 6-8

Prep: 10 minutes Cook: 10 minutes

In a large sauce pan, heat rice syrup and almond butter over low-heat until creamy. Stir in chocolate chips until melted. Remove from heat, stir in cereal until coated and then press into shallow square casserole dish. Allow to set until firm.

Delicious Brownie Cake

1 ½	cups garbanzo beans (canned or cooked)
¾	cup chocolate chips
3	free-range eggs
¾	cup Sucanat
¼	cup butter (1/2 stick)
1	teaspoon baking powder
¼	teaspoon sea salt
¼	teaspoon vanilla

Servings: 6-8

Prep: 25 minutes   Cook: 3-4 hours

Preheat oven to 350°F. Drain and rinse garbanzo beans and process in a food processor into small pieces. Add remaining ingredients and process again until smooth. Pour into a buttered 8 X 8 inch Pyrex dish. Bake at 350°F for about 30 minutes (use a toothpick to determine that it is cooked). Cool cake and frost, if desired.

Serving Suggestions: *Frost with Chocolate-Fudgy Frosting (page 147) and/or top with chopped strawberries.*

Chocolate-Fudgy Frosting

2   tablespoons heavy cream, yogurt, or almond milk
¼   cup Sucanat
¼   cup chocolate chips
1   tablespoon butter
¼   cup raw almond butter or cashew butter

Servings: 1-8X8 cake

Prep: 5 minutes   Cook: 8 minutes

Combine the cream, Sucanat, chocolate chips, and butter
in a heavy saucepan. Stir over medium heat until melted
and mixture comes almost to a boil. Add the nut butter and
mix well. Let cool for 5 minutes before spreading on cake
(has a fudge-like consistency).

Appendix A
Celiac Disease and Other Gluten-Free Resources

Celiac Disease Resources

There are many organizations or groups that are available to support people with celiac disease. Many of these groups are also good for people who are gluten sensitive. They give ideas, recipes, and product suggestions for living a gluten-free lifestyle. Several have very useful newsletters you can sign up for.

Organizations

Celiac Sprue Research Foundation: Science driven public charity that seeks to improve the quality of life of celiac sprue patients. Visit http://www.celiacsprue.org

Celiac Sprue Association: A non-profit support organization dedicated to helping individuals with celiac disease and dermatitis herpetiformis and their families worldwide through research, education, and support. Visit http://www.csaceliacs.org

Celiac Disease Foundation: Provides support, information, and assistance to people affected by celiac disease or dermatitis herpetiformis. Visit http://www.celiac.org

Celiac Disease and Gluten-Free Resource: Provides important resources and information for people on gluten-free diets due to celiac disease, gluten intolerance, dermatitis herpetiformis, wheat allergy, or other health reasons. Visit www.celiac.com

Gluten Intolerance Group (GIG) of North America: Provides support to persons with gluten intolerances, including celiac disease, dermatitis herpetiformis, and other gluten sensitivities, in order to help them lead healthy lives. Visit http://www.gluten.net

American Autoimmune Related Diseases Association: Has information on autoimmune diseases including celiac disease. Visit http://www.aarda.org

Food Allergy & Anaphylaxis Network (FAAN): Has information on ingredient changes, mislabeling, or poor manufacturing practices, as well as other useful food allergy information. Visit http://www.foodallergy.org

Education and Research Centers

Celiac Center at Beth Israel Deaconess Medical Center

http://bidmc.harvard.edu/display.asp?node_id=7031

Celiac Disease Center at Columbia University

http://www.celiacdiseasecenter.columbia.edu/CF-HOME.htm

Celiac Disease Clinic at Mayo Clinic

http://www.mayoclinic.org/celiac-disease/

University of Chicago Celiac Disease Program

http://www.celiacdisease.net/

University of Maryland Center for Celiac Research

http://www.celiaccenter.org/

Support Groups

Visit www.celiac.com to find a support group in your area. Support groups all over the world are listed on this site.

Newsletters

Scott-Free: Provides important articles and information relevant to people on gluten-free diets. Visit http://www.glutenfreemall.com which is powered by http://www.celiac.com

Gluten-Free Baking and More: Dedicated to gluten-free baking, cooking, product reviews, discussions, and more. Visit http://www.glutenfreebakingandmore.com

Jewish Celiacs: Dedicated to the issue of gluten-free kosher foods. Visit www.jewishceliacs.com

Magazines

Gluten-Free Living: A magazine to guide and support people transitioning to a gluten-free lifestyle. Visit http://www.glutenfreeliving.com

Living Without: A lifestyle guide for people with allergies and food sensitivities. It discusses a variety of health-related issues, and provides support and guidance. Visit http://www.livingwithout.com/

Gluten-freeda: An online cooking magazine for people who have celiac disease, and gluten and wheat intolerance. Visit http://www.glutenfreeda.com

Books

Dangerous Grains, by James Braly, M.D., and Ron Hoggan, M.A.

Gluten-Free Diet, A Comprehensive Resource Guide, by Shelley Case, RD

The Gluten Connection - How Gluten Sensitivity May be Sabotaging Your Health, by Shari Lieberman, PhD, CNS, FACN

Against the Grain: The Slightly Eccentric Guide to Living Well Without Gluten or Wheat, by Jax Peters Lowell

Celiac Disease—A Hidden Epidemic, Dr. Peter H.R. Green

Books by Connie Sarros

Books by Bette Hagman

Books by Carol Fenster

Children's Books

Eating Gluten-Free with Emily, Bonnie J. Kruszka

Gluten-Free Friends, An Activity Book for Kids, by Nancy Patin Falini, MA, RD, LDN

Incredible Edible Gluten–Free Food for Kids, Sheri L. Sanderson

Kids with Celiac Disease, Danna Korn who founded Raising Our Celiac Kids (R.O.C.K.), a support group for families of children with celiac disease.

The GF Kid, by Melissa London and Eric Glickman

Appendix B

Gluten-Free Start-Up Shopping Guide

NOTE: You can print a handy PDF version of this Gluten-Free Start-Up Shopping Guide at www.aplacetobe.com

Always Read Labels

Do *not* purchase foods that contain: barley, malt, malt flavoring or malt vinegar, rye, triticale, or wheat *in any form* (durum, graham, kamut, semolina, or spelt included). Also, *avoid* foods that *may* contain gluten such as breading, cereals, gravies, ice cream, imitation foods, licorice, marinades, pastas, processed meats, sauces, soy sauce, soups, stuffing, and thickeners.

Wheat-Free Does *Not* Mean Gluten-Free

Just because a product is wheat-free does *not* mean it is free of gluten items such as rye or barley. Only purchase items that say they are gluten-free.

Be Wary Of Cross Contamination

Keep all gluten-free foods separate from those that are not. Be careful how gluten-free foods are prepared, whether you do it yourself or purchase it somewhere else where cross contamination is possible.

Foods You *Can* Eat

All *plain* meats, poultry, fish, and eggs, corn and rice *in all forms*, legumes and nuts, all *plain* fruits and veggies, dairy products, vegetable oils, vinegar (except for malt), and usually anything that says it is gluten-free.

Acceptable Grain Substitutes

Rice, potato, corn, tapioca, nut flours, beans, garfava, millet, sorghum, quinoa, buckwheat, arrowroot, teff, amaranth, and Montina.

Distilled Alcohols And Wine Can Be Consumed

Gin, whiskey, and vodka do not contain gluten after the distillation process. Wines are also gluten-free, but beers, ales and lagers are not. Note: Some beers are gluten-free

When In Doubt, Bring It Yourself

If you do not know if the places you are going will have foods that you can eat, make sure to have a handy bag or cooler filled with snacks to take with you.

Appendix C
Restaurant Guide
NOTE: You can print a handy PDF version of this Restaurant Guide at www.aplacetobe.com

<u>Research And Always Call Ahead</u>

Doing research online or within your support group will help in selecting gluten-free restaurants. Call ahead to find out if your restaurant choice can cater to your dietary needs. Avoid busy restaurants and fast food restaurants that may not have time to cater to you.

<u>Speak To The Chef</u>

Speak with the chef about options that can be made gluten-free and to ensure your food will be cooked on clean surfaces and with clean utensils.

<u>Explain Your Dietary Restrictions</u>

Say something like "I am on a medically restricted diet and need to avoid grains such as wheat, rye, barley, and any items that have touched or that may contain these grains. Can you or the chef help me in ordering my meal today?"

Items You Can Order

Stick to simple items such as grilled meat, fish, or poultry and a side of steamed vegetables, which are items least likely to be contaminated. Also, salads with lemon juice, oil, and vinegar (no croutons!) are also usually safe to order.

Items To Avoid

Avoid imitation foods, breads, croutons, seasonings, dressings, marinades, soups, fried, and breaded items that may have gluten in them.

Confirm Your Order Before Eating

Be sure to double check with your server that your meal was prepared without any gluten and in a clean area to ensure you do not accidentally get unsafe food.

Be Patient And Express Gratitude

Many servers are not familiar with gluten-free diets, so it is important to be patient when explaining your needs. If you have a successful dining experience, gratitude can go a long way!

About the Authors

David Brownstein, M.D.

David Brownstein, M.D. is a board-certified, family physician that utilizes the best of conventional and alternative therapies. He is the Medical Director for the Center for Holistic Medicine in West Bloomfield, MI. He is a graduate of the University of Michigan and Wayne State University School of Medicine. Dr. Brownstein is board certified by the American Academy of Family Physicians. He is a member of the American Academy of Family Physicians and the American College for the Advancement in Medicine. He is the father of two beautiful girls, Hailey and Jessica, and is a retired soccer coach. Dr. Brownstein has lectured internationally about his success with using natural items. Dr. Brownstein has authored *Salt Your Way to Health*, *Iodine, Why You Need It, Why You Can't Live Without It 3rd Edition*, *The Miracle of Natural Hormones 3rd Edition*, *Overcoming Thyroid Disorders*, *Overcoming Arthritis*, *Drugs That Don't Work and Natural Therapies That Do*, and *The Guide to Healthy Eating*.

Dr. Brownstein's office is located at:
Center for Holistic Medicine
5821 W. Maple Rd. (Ste. 192)
West Bloomfield, MI 48323
248.851.1600
www.centerforholisticmedicine.com
www.drbrownstein.com

Sheryl Shenefelt, C.N.

Sheryl Shenefelt is a Certified Nutritionist that has a passion for learning and researching about food and nutrition. She lives with her wonderful husband Bob, and beautiful children, Grace and Nicholas. Sheryl's interest in health and nutrition peaked even further when she became pregnant with her now 6 year old daughter and with the desire to raise a healthy family. Sheryl currently consults with people individually as well as teaches various classes on nutrition and health at The Center for Holistic Medicine (with Dr. Brownstein) in West Bloomfield, Michigan. She also does "Shop with Sheryl" classes to teach people how to shop for healthy foods.

For more about Sheryl, her recommended organic, natural, and gluten-free resources, and to sign up for her free nutrition e-newsletter, please visit her website at www.aplacetobe.com.

Books by David Brownstein, M.D.

DRUGS THAT DON'T WORK and NATURAL THERAPIES THAT DO 2007

This book will show you why the most commonly prescribed drugs may not be your best choice. Dr. Brownstein shows why drugs have so many adverse effects. The following conditions are covered in this book: high cholesterol levels, depression, GERD and reflux esophagitis, osteoporosis, inflammation and hormone imbalances. He also gives examples of natural substances that can help the body heal.

See why the following drugs need to be avoided:

- Cholesterol-lowering drugs (statins such as Lipitor, Zocor, Mevacor, and Crestor)
- Antidepressant drugs (SSRI's such as Prozac, Zoloft, Celexa, Paxil)
- Antacid drugs (H-2 blockers and PPI's such as Nexium, Prilosec, and Zantac)
- Osteoporosis drugs (Bisphosphonates such as Fosomax and Actonel, Zometa, and Boniva)
- Anti-inflammatory drugs (Celebrex, Vioxx, Motrin, Naprosyn, etc)
- Synthetic Hormones (Provera and Estrogen)

IODINE: WHY YOU NEED IT, WHY YOU CAN'T LIVE WITHOUT IT, 3rd EDITION 2007

Iodine is the most misunderstood nutrient. Dr. Brownstein shows you the benefit of supplementing with iodine. This new edition has three NEW chapters. Iodine deficiency is rampant. Iodine deficiency is a world-wide problem and is at near epidemic levels in the United States. Most people wrongly assume that you get enough iodine from iodized salt. Dr. Brownstein convincingly shows you why it is vitally important to get your iodine levels measured. He shows you how iodine deficiency is related to:

- Breast cancer
- Hypothyroidism and Graves' disease
- Autoimmune illnesses
- Chronic Fatigue and Fibromyalgia
- Cancer of the prostate, ovaries, and much more!

SALT YOUR WAY TO HEALTH 2006

Dr. Brownstein dispels many of the myths of salt. Salt is bad for you. Salt causes hypertension. These are just a few of the myths Dr. Brownstein tackles in this book. He shows you how the right kind of salt--unrefined salt--can have a remarkable health benefit to the body. Refined salt is a toxic, devitalized substance for the body. Unrefined salt is a necessary ingredient for achieving your optimal health. See how adding unrefined salt to your diet can help you:

- Maintain a normal blood pressure
- Balance your hormones
- Optimize your immune system
- Lower your risk for heart disease
- Overcome chronic illness

OVERCOMING THYROID DISORDERS *2004*

This book provides new insight into why thyroid disorders are frequently undiagnosed and how best to treat them. The holistic treatment plan outlined in this book will show you how safe and natural remedies can help improve your thyroid function and help you achieve your optimal health.

- Detoxification
- Diet
- Graves' Disease
- Hashimoto's Disease
- Hypothyroidism
- And Much More!!

THE MIRACLE OF NATURAL HORMONES, 3RD EDITION *2003*

Optimal health cannot be achieved with an imbalanced hormonal system. Dr. Brownstein's research on bioidentical hormones provides the reader with a plethora of information on the benefits of balancing the hormonal system with bioidentical, natural hormones. This book is in its third edition. This book gives actual case studies of the benefits of natural hormones.

See how balancing the hormonal system can help:

- Arthritis and autoimmune disorders
- Chronic fatigue syndrome and fibromyalgia
- Heart disease
- Hypothyroidism
- Menopausal symptoms
- And much more!

OVERCOMING ARTHRITIS *2001*

Dr. Brownstein shows you how a holistic approach can help you overcome arthritis, fibromyalgia, chromic fatigue syndrome, and other conditions. This approach encompasses the use of:

- Allergy elimination
- Detoxification
- Diet
- Natural, bioidentical hormones
- Vitamins and minerals
- Water

THE GUIDE TO HEALTHY EATING *2006*

Which food do you buy? Where should you shop? How do you prepare food? This book will answer all of these questions and much more. Dr. Brownstein co-wrote this book with his nutritionist, Sheryl Shenefelt, C.N. Eating the healthiest way is the most important thing you can do. This book contains recipes and information on how best to feed your family. See how eating a healthier diet can help you:

- Avoid chronic illness
- Enhance your immune system
- Improve your family's nutrition

Call 1-888-647-5616 or send a check or money order to:

Medical Alternatives Press
4173 Fieldbrook
West Bloomfield, MI 48323

All BOOKS $15!

Sales Tax: For Michigan residents, please add $.90 per book.

Shipping:		
	1-2 Books	$5.00
	3-4 Books:	$4.00
	5-7 Books:	$3.00
	8 Books: FREE SHIPPING!	

VOLUME DISCOUNTS AVAILABLE. CALL 1-888-647-5616 FOR MORE INFORMATION OR ORDER ONLINE AT: WWW.DRBROWNSTEIN.COM

NOTE: LECTURE DVD'S ALSO AVAILABLE ONLINE